The Old Me
and
A New i

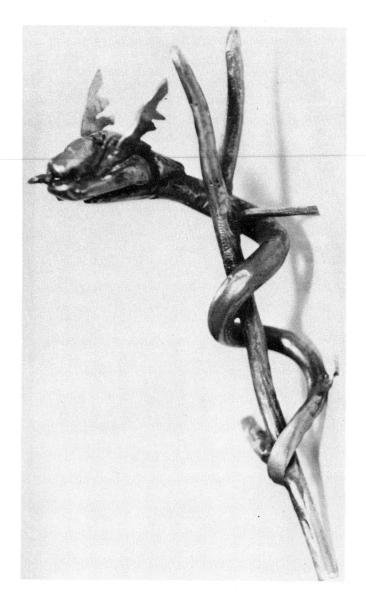

"Then the Lord sent fiery serpents among the people, and they bit the people, so that many people of Israel died." *Numbers 21:6*

The Old Me and A New i

An Exploration of Personal Identity

James B. Ashbrook

JUDSON PRESS, VALLEY FORGE

THE OLD ME AND A NEW I

Copyright © 1974
Judson Press, Valley Forge, PA 19481

Library of Congress Cataloging in Publication Data

Ashbrook, James B   1925-
   The old me and a new i.

   Includes bibliographical references.
   1. Identification (Religion) I. Title.
BV4509.5.A83   248'.4   73-16785
   ISBN 0-8170-0630-3

Printed in the U.S.A.

To Pat
who has lived with
and loved
my old me
while encouraging
and enlivening
my new i

Contents

The Old Me

One   My Several Selves   13

Two   Adam-and-Eve and Me-and-You   27

To Be An i

to be an i   43

Three   To Be An i—as a woman   45

Four   To Be An i—as a man   59

Five   To Be An i—as a human   73

i Yet Not I

Six   Getting My i Together   85

Seven   Giving My i Away   97

Eight   Affirming the Unexpected   107

Preface

My consuming fascination with the issue of identity has taken me in many directions.

Looking back, I see first a passionate concern with injustice on the larger social scene: individuals and groups denied meaning in life by virtue of their being denied the means of life.

Gradually, and imperceptibly, I come upon my own latent longing to be a person of substance and spirit: an individual struggling to be individual.

Subsequently, I experience an intermingling of the social and the personal, of power and presence, of will and love: humanity present in every situation by virtue of the presence of human beings.

I have touched upon some of these personally shaping experiences in an earlier book, *In Human Presence—HOPE*. I have "played with" the pain and the possibilities of a genuine human community in my first book, *be/come Community*. I have explored in more methodical detail and with a broader human focus the perplexity of our not being the human beings that we are in *Humanitas: human becoming and being human*.

Here I attempt to address more simply *and* more biblically the persisting issue of personal identity.

The polarity of Jewish prayer, according to Abraham Heschel in *Man's Quest for God*, has provided the scaffolding of the book's structure: outburst and order, spontaneity and regularity. Certain books have provided a thematic trail for me: Erich Fromm, *Man for Himself;* Paul Tillich, *The Courage to Be;* Rollo May, *Man's Search for Himself;* and Stephen Neil, *A Genuinely Human Existence.* These are a few among many. But books have served primarily as an impetus for more direct personal involvement in my own and others' search for genuine humanness.

I want to express personal and deep appreciation to Neva Reitz, who was inspired as a result of my exploration of the meaning of the serpent to have a serpent on a staff sculptured specifically for me. Lon Foltman photographed the sculpture in a variety of ways, which enabled me to select the views that are used in the book to help convey my intent. Their care and creativity mean much.

You will find that again and again I return to the experience of the seeking self, the centering personality, the dynamic wholeness of the truly human individual; for in truth, the more one is one's full self the less one is one's own self. To become what one is is to be what all are: fully and truly human.

So, I have written with the compelling conviction of "i yet not I

JAMES B. ASHBROOK

The Old Me

to have a self
to be a self
is the greatest concession made to humanity,
but
at the same time
it is
eternity's demand
upon us.
Soren Kierkegaard

Therefore, as it seems,
it is the greatest of all disciplines
to know oneself;

for when one knows oneself,
one knows God.
Clement of Alexandria[1]

ONE
My Several Selves

"...and who are you?"

Ours has become known as "The Identity Society."[2] Human energy, while still geared to survival necessities, is directed more and more to significant needs.

Who we are and what we want command the center of the stage of the human drama.

To write in the first person plural, however, obscures the impact of the identity demand. While the issue eventually must be engaged in terms of our corporate identity—"we"—the issue initially and ultimately is encountered in terms of our unique individual identities—"I." Thus I turn to Lewis Carroll's imaginative portrayal of our human situation. For in describing Alice, Carroll is describing you and me. Her experience conveys our experience:[3]

13

"I've got to grow up again! Let me see: how is it to be managed? I suppose I ought to eat or drink something or other, but the great question is, what?"

The great question certainly was, what? Alice looked all round her at the flowers and the blades of grass, but could not see anything that looked like the right thing to eat under the circumstances. There was a large mushroom near her, about the same height as herself, and when she had looked under it, and on both sides of it, and behind it, it occurred to her to look and see what was on the top of it.

She stretched herself up on tiptoe, and peeped over the edge of the mushroom,

and her eyes immediately met those of a large blue caterpillar, which was sitting with its arms folded, quietly smoking a long hookah, and taking not the least notice of her or of anything else.

For some time they looked at each other in silence : at last the caterpillar took the hookah out of its mouth, and languidly addressed her.

"Who are you?" said the caterpillar.

This was not an encouraging opening for a conversation : Alice replied rather shyly, "I — I hardly know, sir, just at present — at least I know who I _was_ when I got up this morning, but I think I must have been changed several times since that."

"What do you mean by that?" said the caterpillar, "explain yourself!"

"I ca'nt explain _myself_, I'm afraid, sir,"

said Alice, "because I'm not myself, you see."

"I don't see", said the caterpillar.

"I'm afraid I can't put it more clearly," Alice replied very politely, "for I can't under-stand it myself, and really to be so many different sizes in one day is very confusing."

"It isn't," said the caterpillar.

"Well, perhaps you haven't found it so yet," said Alice, "but when you have to turn into a chrysalis, you know, and then after that into a butterfly, I should think it'll feel a little queer, don't you think so?"

"Not a bit," said the caterpillar.

"All I know is," said Alice, "it would feel queer to me."

"You!" said the caterpillar contemptu-ously, "who are you?"

Which brought them back again to the beginning of the conversation

How do you respond to Alice? What does the caterpillar trigger off in you?

Since we cannot talk directly, let me approach your response with responses others have made to her plea. What they say may be similar to what you feel; what they indicate may differ from what you would indicate. Let's see:

A quiet yet determined young organist gives a very personal response.

> I've got to grow up again, too. The something I must drink is that of knowledge: the food I seek is an acquisition of the sense of a personal identity.
>
> "Who are you?" is a difficult question for me particularly and my response is quite similar to Alice's—shy, unknowing, defensive, and even afraid because I can't put it more clearly.

A man with ten years of business experience seeks "exposure to other than conservative business views," especially to minority groups. He intellectualizes more, yet simultaneously he probes the task of self-discovery more deeply:

> When the problem we are focusing on becomes the self, we are unable to grasp the tangibles of flesh in the reflections of the mirror. To examine the self is a process which is difficult because of biases and defenses. We see what we want to see. We see ourselves as we desire others to see us. Yet we are unable to penetrate to their seeing us. Penetration comes only through the eyes of another person and only after the defense mechanisms have been transcended. Penetration of self comes only through open contact with others and only when we are able to drop our defenses and attempt to recognize objectively the manipulations of our lives as experienced by others. We must enter the kingdom of God as a child—openly!

A quiet yet outspoken man who wants others to know that "I'm a person and we probably won't always agree," pours out a much stronger personal reaction:

> WORDS . . .
> WORDS . . .

WORDS . . .

BEAUTIFUL WORDS—MEANINGLESS . . .

Alice really is in Wonderland . . . and so are her words . . .
  I live in a real world . . . a cruel, hateful world bent on
  destroying itself to save itself from humanity.

Who am I? I am who I am—no words.

Who are you? My God—no words.

Define your life—with words.

Define your faith—with words.

  . . . with WORDS?

    WORDS - - - STERILE . . .

    BEGGING FOR A STERILE INTELLECTUAL
    DISCUSSION - - - BREEDING
    ONLY STERILITY

  I live in a real world . . . a cruel, hateful world bent on
  destroying itself to save itself from humanity . . .

and you want a response

to WORDS—

    sterile, meaningless, false,
    beautiful wonderland words

  RESPONSE - - - IMPOSSIBLE

  In the world, the cruel, hateful world—in it I live and move
  and have my being . . .

    RESPONSE IS LIVE - - -
    not written about words.

A pastor of a rural church responds positively. He hopes for growth, even though it may be painful:

My first impression is very favorable. I might even contess to being somewhat excited about the possibilities.

It is no real comfort to realize that I am like most persons in that I am a mixed bag of fear, pride, selfishness, love—and on down the long line of paradoxical traits. I want to be able to make a little more sense of it all.

I am not expecting miracles. I do not expect to receive a simple formula that will forever keep the conflicting feelings in proper order and from henceforth live happily ever after! No, I must confess that I fear this may be a painful experience, but I also feel if I am capable of enduring the pain it will also be a very profitable one!

18

A biology major, somewhat slow in responding, "reluctant to commit" himself, touches upon his panic:

> I find myself identifying with Alice in her dilemma. How does one face "humanness"? The immediate reaction is to run from situations in which one is asked to define his existence and to validate the reason for his being.

A mother, experiencing that painful transition (for women) from the twenties to the thirties, comes seeking growth as an individual and encounters danger—contradiction of cherished values and anxious withdrawal:

> The encounter between Alice and the caterpillar might be called an encounter between parent and child. The child is not sure who she is; she is constantly growing and changing. The caterpillar is secure about who it is, and its indifference to events around it indicates its imperturbability to change. Alice tries to explain herself but can't, because too much has happened to her.
>
> Maybe I might respond in terms of being a parent, in giving over my days as the mother of small children. Pettiness, smallness, develop in me if their concerns are exclusively my concerns, if their world is mine. If as a mother I assume this role too completely, then I run the risk of shutting out other aspects of my personality. If we define our existence in terms of one limited and self-limiting identity, then we lose our true selves which can be evolving processes, not static entities.
>
> I wonder if you have chosen this statement to show that we humans are very much like the caterpillar. We want to sit on our safe little mushroom, with no idea that we can become a beautiful butterfly (a very appropriate symbol of the soul), and fly away free.
>
> But why, having responded to these statements, am I afraid to trust my response to their enormous implications? I retreat and dispassionately regard them as academic.

19

A man headed for the parish ministry reports that he has "fooled" himself into believing what he has often said about himself. From that initial insight he presses further:

Alice's adventure is the story of a child's* encounter with life. What is life but one continuous demand? "If I've got to grow up again. . . . I know who I *was* when I got up this morning, but I think I must have been changed several times since that. . . . I can't explain *myself*, I'm afraid, sir, because I'm not myself, you see." The demand of life causes Alice to realize that need to grow, to become, to "stretch herself up on tiptoe."

This is the world in which we live. It is not the best of all possible worlds as explained by some. It is the *perfect* world— perfect because it (possibly God) drives man to his best; drives him to become. East of Eden is where man lives: on the desert where he must struggle and where he can only eat by the sweat of his brow. It is here that we are shaken from *our* very foundations and cry out with Alice, "I know who I *was* this morning, but NOW I'm not myself!" The greatest accomplishment of the struggle is not the final solution of the problems but *man's growing sense of becoming* which grows out of man's encounter with the struggle. We are driven to "stretch up on tiptoe," to be faced by the constant reality of the large blue caterpillar who asks the ultimate question, "Who are you?"

We find ourselves perplexed, troubled, disturbed to the point that we can only reply rather shyly, "I hardly know." No sympathy do we receive from the caterpillar for he only continues to irritate us with more questions which drive us to our wit's end. It is then, however, when we begin to grow, to become. We cease being children for we have eaten from the tree of knowledge and now we are like the gods themselves, knowing the world in which we live and, yes, the answer to the endless question "Who are you?"

If I stretch up on tiptoe and peep over the edge of the cross, will I possibly find an answer instead of a question? That may depend on my reply to that question. I'm often thrilled at the possibility. Do I receive *an answer from you? I think not.* You look somewhat like a caterpillar.

These are fragments of reactions to Alice's dilemma as presented by me. Some are skeptical; a few are piqued; one is outraged.

---

*Not restricting the definition of "child" to one of age but expanding its meaning to all who are in the early states of self-consciousness.

Several are moved; some are stirred; a few are turned on. Clarity and confusion course through their associations.

Do you find your reactions resonating with any of these? Do you experience other associations, different demands, other cares? How are you responding?

"I've got to grow up again!"

"Who wants to?"

For *those of us who have supposedly "made it,"* we're tired of growing. We like—or at least we claim to like—who we are with what we have where we are. All the talk of change only serves to depress us at best or to frighten us at worst.

We know who we are. We do not want to have to struggle with the confusing question of identity. This morning, before the demands of the day, we were confident of who we were.

"We are proud of ourselves; that's what I'd like to say," so declares forty-three-year-old Joe, unintentionally reflecting the attitude of millions of middle America. (Joe was one of many people interviewed by Robert Coles in preparation of his book *The Middle Americans.*) Yet behind the certainty lurks uncertainty. "We're not sure of things, though; we're uncertain, I'm afraid, and when you're like that—worried, it is—then you're going to lose a little respect for yourself. You're not so proud anymore."

Many of us like Joe "don't have time" for directly and unselfconsciously thinking about life's meaning and who one is.

"I'll have to admit, there'll be a few seconds here and there when I'll put them to myself. I'll say, Joe, what's it all about . . . ? I'll ask myself what I want out of life."[4]

Some of us are the forgotten American. We work regularly, steadily, dependably. We wear a blue collar or a white collar; yet the frontiers of our life's expectations have been fixed since we reached the age of thirty-five. We find we have too many obligations, too much family, and too few skills to match what we find with what we hope. We do all the right things. We obey the law. We go to church. We insist—usually—that our kids get a better education than we had.[5]

"But the right things don't seem to be paying off."

All the rules are changing, and we feel stranded. Our sure sense of self shudders from the shock of the future right here, right now.

We are tired of struggling. We want peace and quiet—the garden, the television, the comfort of the familiar, the reassurance of agreement. Why can't we stay the way we are—or at least keep the hope of the way we want to be? Why do we have to grow again?

Thus is the fear in those of us who felt sure of who we were. Our ideas of right and wrong, our expectations of what mattered, our confidence in home and school and church and government—all served us well but now leave us ill. If we are not sure of who we are, we are at least insistent as to who we are *not*. We are *not* black or red or brown or unemployed or intellectual or hippies or members of the drug scene or rich or professional people or big businessmen or well-born or well-to-do or well-educated.[6]

But as ordinary, plain, average people, how acutely we feel left out, abused, ignored, enraged, confused. We thought we knew who we were. Now we find we've got to grow again. Now we've got to face again the perplexing question of who we are.

Others of us are well able to influence what goes on around us. One such man dreamed: "I am in a great assembly. In the center of the room is a circular space . . . where a man is seated, writing the names of the people who enter. I see myself walking rather majestically through the crowd, and as I reach the gate I proudly give my name in a loud voice—'Head of Fifty-seven Committees.'"[7] Clothed in the dress of respectability and responsibility, this dreamer experiences himself only in terms of what he does. There is no reference to the reality of who he is.

Yet the very assurance of the dream suggests the inner strain. The more we insist upon our importance the less significant we feel, for behind the facade of confidence lurks the fear of emptiness and even nothingness. As the apostle Paul warned, "If you feel sure that you are standing firm, beware! You may fall." (1 Corinthians 10:12, NEB)

Here, for instance, is a woman who married her brother's best friend right after college. For the next period of years she lived comfortably as the wife of an oil company executive and as the mother of two children in a suburban community.

22   "I gardened and served and cooked and had a Girl Scout troop and was a Cub Scout mother and belonged to committees of the PTA," she acknowledged. "Outwardly I was a mature, well-adjusted person. But I was dead."[8]

It is that "dead" quality that haunts many of us in the rushing days and restless nights. As another very outgoing woman dreamed: "I had cut myself up and was passing myself round on a large and handsome platter. At first there was nothing unusual about it, but suddenly I became terrified and tried to pull away the platter and escape, but I could not move or speak. . . ."[9] She had thrown herself into so many and such varied activities that she had little or no self left by the end of the day. She had given herself away in bits and pieces. People had walked off with her, leaving her with no-body.

For *many of us more comfortable Americans* what we have relied on no longer seems reliable. What we have invested in no longer seems worthwhile. What we have supposed ourselves to be no longer makes much sense. By reinforcing a single view of ourselves we have turned ever more rigid and ever more fragile.

"It is a short, short road from Teensville to Squarestown," observes Charles Reich in *The Greening of America.* "Soon [young people's] senses have been dulled, their strength put under restraint, their minds lobotomized; bodies still young, cut off from selves, walk the windowless, endless corridors of the Corporate State."[10]

Even more terrifying, *some of us excluded Americans* have been driven to disparage and deny the very selves we are.

In Pittsburgh a four-year-old black girl stood in front of a mirror scrubbing her skin with soap. When diverted, she scrubbed the mirror. When urged to paint instead, she angrily covered sheets of paper with brown and black. Eventually she brought the teacher "a really *good* picture."[11] It was covered completely with white!

How tragically deep runs the identity disturbance precipitated in those of us made to feel so decidedly different.

Let's look at this in terms of drawings by a black girl in Mississippi. These are taken from investigations by Robert Coles which he reports in a book entitled *Children of Crisis.*[12] Ruby was six years old when Coles first met her. She drew white people larger and more lifelike and black people smaller and more distorted.

On the right on the next page you see a picture of Ruby by Ruby. Notice how her left arm is shorter than her right. There are only two fingers. On the right hand there are only four fingers. There is little substance to her body. The colors are drab. In Ruby's pictures her own face often lacked an eye or an ear; yet the faces of whites never did.

Figure 2
A white girl by Ruby at age 6

Figure 1
Ruby by Ruby at age 6

On the left you see a picture of a white classmate, which Ruby drew at the same time. Notice how solid the girl is. She has a body. Look at her arms; they are developed. Each hand has five fingers. The feet have toes. The flowers are colorful. The sun is shining.

This is the way Ruby saw her world—herself and others. These are the images she carried around in her head of what she was like.

The crisis in black identity has served to sharpen the crisis in everyone's identity.

"There are times," middle-American Joe confessed, "when I feel like a nigger myself; I'll admit it. I've been going all day, and I'm back at work after supper . . . and I'll say to myself: Joe, you're a goddamn slave, that's what you are; you might as well be picking cotton or something like that." [13]

It is not just blacks: it's women; it's men; it's browns; it's reds; it's yellows; it's whites; it's old; it's young; it's ins; it's outs—it's everyone—everyone as *nigger!*

Life has come to the point where we are so many, we move so fast, we live so close, and we are so varied that no one feels right about what one is, where one is, and with whom one lives any longer. How many of us experience uncertainty as to who we are! We are all hard pressed, weary, frustrated, fragmented, frightened. Instead of our being together, we find ourselves apart.

There are some of us—really very few of us, the rare exceptions, I believe—who are both confident of and content with who we are. Affluence and adequacy shield us from the upheavals in society. It is as though we stand on the sandy beach (not yet washed away by the storm—cf. Matthew 7:24-27) and listen to the agonizing cries of those not-so-distant swimmers who are drowning. We shout to them to swim. All they have to do is move their arms and legs, thrash around, head for shore. What's the matter with them? Why can't they simply be who they are? What's all the moaning and groaning and gnashing of teeth? If people would just stop arguing and bickering and angling, all this discontent and disruption and disillusionment would disappear.

What we protected (deluded?) people don't realize is that under the water those swimmers' "hands and feet are tied."[14] The drowning people *can't* swim! Anxiety paralyzes movement. Whereas previously individuals could be and were unsettled without unsettling society, now society itself is unsettled and so unsettles individuals. Whereas previously Americans could view themselves as the good guys from the Boston Tea Party to the Nuremberg trial, now we are brought face to face with the horrors of our ignored disturbance—racism; My Lai; sexism; falsification and destruction of official documents involving 100,000 tons of B-52 bombing in Cambodia; secret, sophisticated intelligence surveillances because of political differences; law-and-order transformed into loyalty-at-any-price-by-any-means-for-self-serving-ends Watergate; business manipulations of public interest at home and abroad for private gain. Cultural collapse parallels and reflects individual collapse. The old mess in society mirrors the old me of ourselves.

You remember that dramatic encounter between Jesus and the seriously disturbed man on the shore of the country of the Gerasenes (Mark 5:1-20). The community had rejected him, driven him out of the populated areas, confined him to the deserted regions. He ran naked, yelling, screaming, bruising himself with rocks. That supposedly sane society had given birth to a supposedly insane human being. It had forgotten the truth that the sickness of society surfaces most acutely in the disturbances of its more sensitive members.

When confronted by Jesus, the tormented man cried out: "What have you to do with me, Jesus, Son of the Most High. For God's sake, don't torture me." That was his response to Jesus' having commanded the evil spirit to come out of him.

Then Jesus asked him, "What is your name? What is your identity? Tell me. Show me. Who are you?"

The man answers, "My name is Legion, for there are many of us."

Whether we meet a caterpillar who unexpectedly upsets us by asking "Who are you?" or whether we are confronted by a turbulent culture that batters us with our inadequate identity, or whether we encounter the caring Christ who would bring us to our senses by demanding to know our name, we cannot avoid the task of being and becoming ourselves.

Birth comes to us as the gift of being. Life confronts us with the demand to become. We have to grow again—and again—and again—and always. . . .

Yet our several selves—our scattered pieces—our brokenness—this is what we have to work with: our kaleidoscopic me's.

"God, when he made man,
made him straightforward,
but man invents endless subtleties of his own."
Ecclesiastes 7:29, NEB

TWO
Adam-and-Eve and Me-and-I

How has it come about?

We, who are the pinnacle of the evolutionary pyramid (according to Genesis 1), so often and so furiously tear down what we are.

How does it come to pass?

We, who are the center of things (according to Genesis 2 and 3), so often and so violently destroy that center.

How are we to account for it?

We, who have received the gift of the living present, so often and so insistently choose to rehash the dead past or to rehearse an illusory future.

How is it?

Between that gift of being human and that task of human becoming lies the paradox. I use the image of "the old me" as a way of summarizing the dilemma, the paradox, the predicament. Though we were created to be a certain way, we now find ourselves acting in other ways. What was originally so very good (Genesis 1:31) originates so much that is so very bad. What appears to be the best turns out to be the worst (Romans 1:18-23). What was meant for life produces death.

The owner of a gasoline station responds to the frustration of cars lining up to get service. People are racing their motors, looking at their watches, inching up on each other. In conversation with Robert Coles he reflects on human beings: "I think they'd like to push each other onto the road, so they'd get the fast service they want. In this world, everyone wants to push everyone else. It's amazing people *ever* put their feet on the brakes in time."[1]

The fact of the old me confronts us at every moment. That little slice out of a gas owner's reaction to life only points to more universal experience.

Consider some of these experiences as lifted up by biblical writers:

> People found they could not get along (see Genesis 4:1-8; 6:5-7). They talked the same language yet meant different things (see Genesis 11:1-9). They wanted to love yet found themselves fighting (see Genesis 2:18, 21-25; 3:12-13). They intended the best, yet acted their worst (see Genesis 9:20-21). They did what they could, but it was never enough (Romans 3:9-20). The centered self became self-centered (see Genesis 3:7-12). Self-actualization turned into self-deification (see Genesis 3:22-24). Even before they had a chance to get going, their lives were somehow off-balance (see Genesis 3:14-19).

From the accumulation of these particular kinds of experience, people began to conclude there was something universal in them. Whatever was going on affected everyone, and everyone affected whatever was going on. The old me lifts up, even as it points toward, human life as being off-balance, out-of-order, missing-the-mark or however you care to describe it.

In traditional religious language, I am pointing toward "original sin." We can look at any situation and discover how it is off-balance and out-of-order and missing-the-mark. Such experience is reflected—abstractly—in this picture in which the artist only loosely groups a number of circles without a dominant center or else makes the circles asymmetrical, suggesting the off-balance of our world.[2]

Wherever we look, we can see the crucial part played by conflicting and polarized forces:

—between building up and tearing down
—between conserving and creating
—between being part of the whole and being as oneself

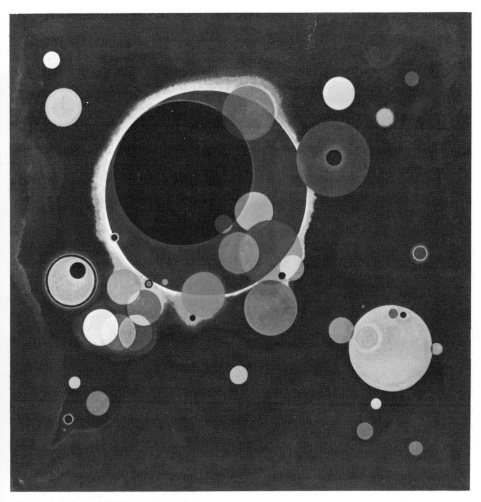

The Solomon R. Guggenheim Museum, New York

29

—between a private inner world and a public outer world
—between having found and still seeking

What we are about—that is, making and keeping life truly human—requires starting where we are; that is, seeing tension, conflict, anxiety, polarization—the old me. We cannot be responsible for the off-balance before we arrived on the scene. We *are* responsible for the off-balance now that we are here.

The step from what we find to what we shape moves the focus from "original sin" to the experience of "sin." We shift from seeing only what happens to us to seeing how we in turn happen to it. The issue of sin leads us to look more concretely at the ways we are throwing the weight of our lives into unbalancing specific situations.

It is this quality of our personal participation in what happens that led a theologian like Tillich to retain the word "sin." [3] He had great difficulty with its moralistic overtones. He rejected its endless list of special acts. In the end, though, he claimed that the word could and must be saved. There is a sharpness in the word which accuses us of personal responsibility for the human mess.

The doctrine of original sin reminds us to take account of the drag of humankind. We do not begin life in a vacuum. Because humanity does not begin with each new baby, though each baby means a fresh start, "the sinfulness of the race acquires a history." In truth, Kierkegaard went on, "Original sin is growing." [4] We are born into a situation that is already off-balance. That initial imbalance upsets our balance. Our imbalance then multiplies the total imbalance of humanity.

We find ourselves in a situation which, as theologian Albert Outler put it, is "unstable at best and disastrous at worst." [5] Parents injure their children with their own anxieties. Society injures parents and children with its complexities and conflicts. Institutional racism and the bondage of women painfully symbolize the power of structures to shape us despite our best intentions.

We do not need to subscribe to the biological tainting of St. Augustine's theory of original sin. We need only look to the psychological, sociological, ecological, and spiritual warping that each generation inflicts upon its progeny. The sins of the fathers *are* visited upon the children unto the third and fourth generations (Exodus 20:5-6).

Our ability to respond is not only restricted by the drag of the race, but we are equally restricted by the drag of ourselves. Depth psychology simply emphasizes and elaborates what Augustine, Luther, Paul, and others saw. At the core of the person is an irrational and irresponsible quality. Our best possibilities are somehow, again to quote Outler, always a "compromise between unlimited desire and limited satisfaction." [6] Even when we act in the most authentic way, we stumble over ambiguous elements of fitting and unfitting, health and sickness, caring and competing, loving and hating, helping and harming. As Ishmael declares in *Moby Dick:* "Heaven have mercy on us all—Presbyterians and Pagans alike—for we are all somehow dreadfully cracked about the head, and sadly need mending." [7]

That mysterious intermingling of situation and self found humorous description in Shirley Jackson's delightful account of her family, *Life Among the Savages.* One morning, as she and her husband lay peacefully in bed, she heard the children singing. At first she thought how nice that they were getting along. Then she heard the words—"Baby ate a spider, Baby ate a spider."

In a flash she flew out of bed, down the hall, and burst into the room. The children were jumping up and down obviously elated and excited—until they saw their mother's face.

"What did you eat?" she demanded of baby Sally, who was peering through the bars of her crib and grinning broadly. "What do you have in your mouth?"

Twelve-year-old Laurie, in his cowboy-print pajamas, shouted triumphantly from the top of the dresser where he was beating time with a coat hanger: "A spider," he said. "She ate a spider."

Shirley Jackson forced open the baby's mouth. It was empty. "Did she *swallow* it?"

"Why?" asked young Jannie, sitting on her bed in pink pajama pants. "Will it make her sick?"

By this time Laurie realized all was not well. He quickly sought to recover his position. *"Jannie* gave it to her."

By this time Jannie realized all was not well. She quickly sought to recover her position. *"Laurie* found it."

Finally, in desperation Laurie hastily declared, "But she ate it herself." [8]

Baby Sally had not been responsible for setting up the situation of the spider. However, once the situation was there, she was the one who responded. No one could swallow it for her. Only she could do that for herself.

George Jackson, in one of his prison letters to his father in *Soledad Brother,* expressed such intermixture of messed-up setting and a self that shares in the mix-up:

> Though I know I am a victim of social injustice and economic pressure and though I understand the forces that work to drive so many of our kind (black) to places like this and to mental institutions, I can't help but know that I proceeded wrong somewhere.[9]

As Luther insisted, the most personal acts one always does for oneself. No one can be baptized for me; no one can believe for me; no one can die for me. Only I can respond to the situation in which I find myself. While I am not responsible for the situation before I am there, once here I respond. And that response *is* my responsibility!

How did all this messy me and messy world come about? Or, to put the question positively, how do we humans get to be human? From whence comes the old me? On what can we count for a new i?

For myself, the Hebraic experience of being and becoming human offers the richest source of understanding. It starts from unqualified affirmation while simultaneously exposing perplexing ambiguity. Human perplexity—the old me—comes from our assertion against the will of the good God. Humanity revolts against its own Humanity, being against Being, thereby invoking judgment. The Hebrews took a critically positive view of life.

It is to this critical yet positive view of who we are that I want to direct your attention.

In the book of Genesis we are given intuitive insight into human creation and human complications. This has been taken by many as literal history, by others as meaningless fantasy. In fact, this is Priestly Doctrine—that is, in the creation accounts we have ancient and sacred knowledge, which had been handed on by countless generations, each pondering what it received, reformulating it, and passing it on as living experience. The doctrine, thus, while objectified historical expression, still retains the roots of shared personal experience. Because the material has been reworked through the centuries, every trace of private idiosyncracies has vanished.[10] In their stead we are given public and universal understanding, revelation, if you will.

The birth of humanity—of personhood, of selfhood—is por-

32

trayed in the two creation stories (Genesis 1:1–2:4a; 2:4b–3:24). Each of these accounts focuses on different human questions. Together they present us with a composite of the felt-meaning of the human situation.

In contrast to other views of creation, the Hebrews find the clue to human being and becoming more in actual events than in natural processes. Their understanding of YHWH—the Nameless Name—comes from what happened to them more than from the cosmos in which they found themselves. (In Hebrew, YHWH are the letters often translated "I AM" as in Exodus 3:14.)

Concrete situations and interpersonal relationships disclose the sacred realm. Here is the place of the experienced reality of ultimate meaning. What unfolds historically is taken as God's disclosure of genuinely human existence. Rather than nature's cycle of spring/summer/autumn/winter, the experience of what is meant to be influences our understanding of what life really is. Human freedom stands out more sharply in the experience of the Hebrews than the mere existence of human beings. In short, the knowledge of (the book of) Exodus with its portrayal of liberation from bondage comes prior to the understanding of (the book of) Genesis with its portrayal of creation.[11] History, not nature, provides the key to life.

Well, what did unfold? What might that mean for us? For the Hebrews, two components characterize humanity's developing consciousness of itself:

1. From having been nothing, they found themselves to be something; in effect, creation *ex nihilo*, being-out-of-nothingness. They had been slaves in Egypt; unexplainably they found themselves liberated in the wilderness. What could they make of that? Only that life was on the side of life, the Power of Being broke people out of boxes in the possibility of becoming who they are.

2. Even though they experienced freedom, they continually bumped up against limitation. The limitation of the outer environment of space and time was minor compared with the limitation of the inner world of wishfulness and willfulness, of distortion and disequilibrium.

For Hebraic man, his experience of freedom and limitation had to be accounted for. What should have been easy constantly frustrated. What should have helped continually hurt. What should have been whole invariably fractured. It was to these enigmatic experiences that biblical man articulated his human answer.

How could such bewildering experiences be relatable?

How did such conflicting experiences come about?

What was the link between the universal expression of freedom/limitation and the personal expression of these same qualities?

One way of getting inside these Genesis portrayals of the old me with our fixed actuality and a new i with our open possibilities is to think of them as dreams. I do not mean they are dreams. But dreams are deep symbolic expressions of personal and universal experience. In them we see extensions and expressions of ourselves. The ways we have learned to understand dreams can aid us in understanding biblical meanings,[12] for in the Bible we see extensions and expressions of humanity.

These accounts dramatize the birth of humanity—the bursting forth of selfhood. Each account highlights different aspects of the same experience. They belong together and are finally only understandable together, for they come out of the interplay between the inner depth of felt-meaning and the outer realm of what's-happening. Together they are humanity making sense of itself and its becoming.

PURPOSEFULNESS

What do we learn about ourselves from the sophisticated sweep of chapter 1 in Genesis?

Clearly, life makes sense. It is going somewhere, not just going around in circles. Biblical people could put their trust in life's meaning because the entire historical drama unfolded within the purpose of the God they worshiped as creator and redeemer. Humanity stands at the top of the creation process.

But such height is linked with depth. Always and ever within our orderly world we experience chaos—the constant threat to everything that is. And the affirmation that order comes out of disorder points to the miracle and perpetual miracle of ongoing creation. From the formless abyss of potentiality, God's intention has shaped actual open-ended existence. Creation is a meaningful process of the creation of meaning.

Even though the immediate can never capture nor contain the transcendent, the immediate is never depreciated. There is no

34

forbidden tree; there is no tragic fall. While life as we know it is never the last word, life as we live it is always the necessary fact. While never the greatest good, nevertheless, creation is ever the "very good." Even the terrible monsters of the deep (Genesis 1:21), the powerful impersonal forces of natural vitality, are known as "good." The natural order may be chaotic, but for the liberated that order is neither cancelled nor rejected. Life is ever to be celebrated!

The Hebrew word for "create" (*bara*) means separate—to create is to divide. Yet we can divide precisely because we can trust that life is whole. The first act of creation came when "God said, 'Let there be light'; and there was light" (Genesis 1:3). That means God's first move was the activation of illumination.[13] Awareness of distinctions and differences follows from that initial consciousness.

Light—consciousness—illumination—differentiation—pours in, moving chaos from dread darkness into awakening clarity. The first and primary separation, the basis of all distinctions, is the division of light from darkness, seeing from not seeing.

The text stresses the task of responding more than the gift of being able to respond. Because we are created in the image of God, we are capable of ruling over the whole of creation (Genesis 1:26-31; cf. Genesis 2:19-20a).

But the source of creation as other than ourselves warns us against taking the world as something we can play with as we please. The universe is not at our private disposal—susceptible to the meanings we impose and subject to the purposes we devise. The cosmos is not ours; it is the Other's. The integrity of each part and the integrity of the whole are to be maintained.

Similarly, the goal of creation as ahead rather than behind evokes in us an understanding of what we really are: limited and passing who, together with all that is, are dependent upon life other than our life. Our life derives its meaning from relationship to that Reality that initiates human history and quickens, guides, and corrects it from beginning to end.[14] We are here for the making of one another. To create is to relate.

35

COMPLEXITY

The overview of Genesis 1 suggests the purposeful goodness of creation. What do we learn from the sharper focus of the complementary view in Genesis 2 (and 3)?

Clearly, life is complex. Creation has contrast, polarity, balancing: here/there, this side/that side, God/human, human/world, male/female, outer/inner, now/then, yes/no, separation/union.

The parts are polar. They are the end points in a single reality. What connects them is more basic than the parts themselves.[15] Thus polarization is prevented. The affirmation that creativity comes out of balancing and rebalancing does point toward the mystery and the perpetual mystery of history, for the understanding of Genesis 2 moves not between the poles of stasis and change but between the poles of balancing and fulfilling. From the balancing and counterbalancing changes of history, God is shaping the creative fulfillment of humanity. God transcends humanity in the process of more genuine humanness.

Here humanity is seen at the center of things. This is, as Gerhard von Rad characterizes the experience, "man's world, the world of his life (the sown, the garden, the animals, the woman), which God in what follows establishes *around man*; and this forms the primary theme of the entire narrative, *'ādām, 'adāmā* (man—earth)."[16] In this anthropocentic universe humanity is "the center of a circle."

It is, therefore, the human factor that unites depth and height. It is the human factor that connects distance and closeness. Nature and God are organized around humanity. Humanity organizes what's here.

Astonishing as the idea may be, the story contains the experience of the human becoming of each one of us. The Garden portrays the place of our conception and birth—the womb of our creation. We are forced out of the immediacy of the womb into the remoteness of the world. The birth canal itself is the physiological prototype of the entrance at the East of Eden. Within the womb we are safe. Within the world we experience threat. As individuals, we are at once ourselves and humanity. By analogy, Adam is himself and humanity. Therefore, what explains Adam explains humanity and vice versa.[17]

36

The word "Adam" does not mean a particular person, such as James Ashbrook. The Revised Standard Version translates the word more accurately as "man," which means humankind, generic humanity (Genesis 2:7). I am Adam. You are Adam.

And the word "Eve" does not refer to a particular person, such as Patricia Ashbrook. It implies living, life, mother of every living thing (Genesis 3:20). I am living. You are living.

The story of Adam and Eve is the story of every human being. We find here not only our inbetweenness—you-and-I—but also our individual innerness—me-and-i—Adam-and-Eve.

In the first account of conceiving, man and woman are created simultaneously. In the second they are created sequentially, the woman being derived from man.[18]

In the first account the focus is light—consciousness—creating distinguishable objects. In the second the focus is developing selfhood.

Together, as dream interpretation suggests, the accounts transcend time and space. They elaborate the process of separating and uniting within each one's own developing personality and in relation to the world of people and things.

The Tree of Life has universally stood for life. It symbolizes the mysterious and perpetual regeneration of a human world. On the other hand, the Tree of the Knowledge of Good and Evil is without parallel in ancient expression. Nowhere else were knowledge and life divided.[19] The issue is "*this* tree" of knowledge and not how to get life out of death, as the serpent suggests.[20] The knowledge referred to does not mean moral concepts such as good and bad. Rather, it alludes to universal understanding, an experiencing and becoming intimately acquainted with everything.[21]

The awakening of human awareness constitutes both our human predicament—the old me—*and* our human possibility—a new i. Here we find Adam's order (Genesis 2:19-20a) and Eve's outburst (Genesis 3:6a), Eve's routine and Adam's responsiveness (Genesis 3:6b).

Consciousness itself *is* the act of conception and creation.

Consciousness itself *is* the gulf of separation.

Consciousness itself *is* the bridge of union.

The account portrays humanity's (and therefore your and my) awakening self-consciousness. Conscious choices enter the field of possibility. The field is both positive and negative. As Kierkegaard put it, the possibility of freedom stands out as "the alarming possibility of being able."[22]

What we make of our humanity, if we immerse ourselves in the biblical view, is not a paradise lost and a paradise to be regained.

What we find is the exciting, frustrating, fascinating transition from human potential to human wholeness. We are to seek new creation, not old creation; new being, not old being; a new i, not the old me (2 Corinthians 5:17). We are called forward, never backward. We seek the greatest God that we might become our truest selves.

Genesis 2 lays bare the drama of wholeness. The issue is the transformation of potential wholeness into actual wholeness. In symbolic language, we see unfolding the *human* growth of humanity, outburst and order, structure and spontaneity.

THROWN INTO LIFE

To be thrown into life is to be called upon to respond. We are to make something of what is. No other creature must decide to be part of life. No other creature has to struggle with who it is. No other creature needs to face what it is to be(come).

Only we must decide to be what we are by becoming what we are conceived to become.

Only we hear the question, "Where are you?" (Genesis 3:9-10).

Only we tremble from the threat to who we are because of what we do. "I heard the sound of the truly Other and I was afraid, because I was exposed; and I hid myself."

Only we resort to deception and defensiveness that splits what we do from who we are.

Anxiety floods in. We are seldom sure of what is happening. We sense everything is not right. We know we are off-balance. We find ourselves reacting defensively. We shift responsibility from here to there, from now to then, from us to them, from me to you. We cannot *not* respond.

Traditionally, people have used the Garden of Eden to explain human pride. The Greek word for pride is *hubris,* a kind of unlimited self-elevation. "Eat this and you shall be as God" (Genesis 3:4-5).

More recently, people are using the Garden to explain human sloth. The Greek word for sloth is *acedia,* a kind of indifference or not caring. As Harvey Cox describes it, "Sloth means being *less* than instead of *more* than [human]. Sloth describes our flaccid unwillingness to delight in the banquet of earth or to share the full measure of life's pain and responsibility. It means to abdicate in part or in whole the fullness of one's own humanity."[23]

Our human perplexity embraces both the *hubris* of straining to be more than we are and the *acedia* of being content with less than we are. Like Eve we break out of the boundaries in which we find ourselves; like Adam we withdraw into the securities we have created to protect ourselves.

We want too much;
we give too little.

Today, apathy constitutes the focus of much of our sin. We irresponsibly shift the locus of initiative and involvement and accountability and evaluation from "us" to "them" or "it." Cox terms this irresponsible apathy *acedia*. "For Adam and Eve, apathy meant letting a snake tell them what to do. It meant abdicating ... the exercise of dominion and control over the world. For us it means allowing others to dictate the identities with which we live out our lives."[24]

Traditionally, people have also used the Garden of Eden to highlight lack of faith. Unfaith points to the way we turn from a transcendent center and turn instead to ourselves as THE center. We lose connection with the world. We refuse to trust the trustworthiness of God.

Unfaith is invariably intertwined with concupiscence. *Concupiscence* comes from a Latin word for a kind of unlimited desiring. In unfaith our unlimited desiring for union with that which is beyond turns back upon ourselves. Like Narcissus gazing at himself in the pool, we see only our own reflection. There is no life other than our life, no center other than our center, no truth other than our truth, no love other than our love.

We, then, mistakenly believe that we are alpha and omega, the beginning and the end. Yet we long for larger life. But since we shut ourselves up and cut ourselves off, that intense desiring only results in our devouring ourselves with an insatiable hunger for love or drowning ourselves in our own exaggerated self-consciousness. In concupiscence. we try to draw the whole of reality into our own little reality. Because we do not believe others capable of being responsible, like Adam we depend too much on routine procedures and unquestioned authority. Because we are concerned primarily about ourselves, like Eve we cavalierly barge into situations indifferent to the presence and concerns of others.

We trust too little;
we take too much.

The drive to be(come) the center of everything results in the experience of our ceasing to be the center of anything. Both self and world, centeredness and relatedness, are destroyed. Instead of creativity, there is conformity; regularity curbs spontaneity. Instead of continuity, there is chaos; spontaneity undoes regularity. Instead of exuberance, there is exploitation; order crushes outburst. Instead of affirmation, there is aggression; outburst assaults order.

No one is safe. Nothing is sacred.
Everything collapses. Life breaks down.

Once we are thrown into life, there can be no return to the womb. Consciousness precludes an unbroken immediacy with one's environment. At the east of the Garden/womb (Genesis 3:24) two angels guard the entrance. At the threshold of selfhood we have to move out into the world. Within ourselves we carry *and* must express both the old me and the new i.

The Genesis 2 account of the Lord God creating humanity from the dust of the ground and breathing into our nostrils the breath of life (Genesis 2:7) expresses our human situation. Neither dust nor breath are to be taken literally as substances such as body-substance or soul-substance. Rather they are to be understood experientially as ways of being in the world: we-are-here-with-possibility.[25] We are to maintain and enhance the humanness of our humanity.

Yet the account reminds us that we tend not to be as fully human as we in fact are.

Because we want too much,
we can fail. We can lose our creativity.
We can *not become.*

Because we trust too little,
we can forget we are limited. We can lose
our faith. We can *not be.*

Because we give too little,
we can submerge who we are. We can lose
our power. We can *not be ourselves.*

Because we take too much,
we can cut ourselves off. We can lose
our love. We can *not belong.*
The old me seems to crowd out any new i.

To Be an i

Not "how shall we know?"
but "how shall we live?"

"What is important . . . is that
    our lives
    should be
    as *big* as possible. . . ."

    Each of us
    should become
    a person,

    a whole and integrated person
    in whom there is manifested

        a sense of the human variety
        genuinely experienced,

        a sense of having come to terms
        with a reality
        that is

                awesomely
                  vast.[1]
            Theodore Roszak

"When we were baptised we went into the tomb with him and joined him in death, so that as Christ was raised from the dead by the Father's glory, we too might live a new life."

Romans 6:4, *Jerusalem Bible*

To Be An i

To look at "who I am" in general is to miss "who I am" in particular. Yet much of the passion for liberation—regardless of origin—is only initially "black" liberation or "women's" liberation. Finally, it is always "human" liberation. While I have dealt with the old me somewhat generally—that is, without focusing attention on sex or race or class or age—to have done so is to have obscured the needs and demands specific to various groups of people and certainly to every individual.

Careful investigation of human differences based on sex, to look at one of the most dominant differences, fails to support any simple description of what is peculiarly male and what is peculiarly female.[2] The same confusion applies to descriptions of racial differences, socio-economic or class differences, as well as age differences. Even so, there remains a certain wisdom in taking such differences into account in dealing with identity. We can too easily dismiss or ignore the vitality and richness of differences for the sake of a blind superiority in a majority—and a terrible inferiority in the minorities.

Sameness breeds sterility. Distinctiveness yields abundantly.

The issue, then, is: what aspects of identity do we hold in common and what aspects do we hold separately? Humanness includes both our separate identity as *human* beings and our shared identities as human *beings*.

The predicament of transforming the old me into a new i necessitates looking at our separate identities at this point. In considering "to be an i—as a woman" I deal explicitly with women, while in "to be an i—as a man" I deal explicitly with men.[3] But in terms of full *human* functioning what is distinguishable about females is needed as much in men as what is distinguishable about males is needed in women.

43

To speak quite generally, love and will are basic forces in all of us.[4] Will characterizes our individual experience. As such, it emphasizes aloneness, differences, isolation, initiative, mastery, assertion, distinguishing, and ordering. Love, in contrast, characterizes our communal experience of participating in something other than and larger than ourselves. As such, it discloses contact, openness, union, similarity, integration, cooperation.

In the aggregate, males and females can be distinguished in this way: will being characteristically masculine; love characteristically feminine. In making the point this way, however, we must realize that we are recognizing differences between male and female at the same time we are acknowledging that these forces are active in both men and women.

Will and love are in all of us and in each of us. In fact, finally, we can only speak of specific differences in aptitudes and personality as between men and women, for sex differences are mostly cultural. The overlap in all psychological characteristics is so great that we must consider everyone as an individual more than as a member of a group.

THREE

To Be An i—As A Woman

How does a girl become a woman?

Thus, the question of a new i is asked by women's liberation. It implies the backdrop of the old me of how a girl becomes a gal: pink and frilly clothes, dolls and doll houses—she's quiet and well-balanced, sexy and sexless, devoted and diligent. And—

"A woman's place is in the home/Housewives are such dull people/Women's talk is all chatter/Intelligent women are emasculating/If you're so smart why aren't you married?/Can you type?/If you want to make decisions in this family go out and earn a paycheck yourself/Working women are un-feminine/A smart woman never shows her brains/It is a woman's duty to make herself attractive/All women think about are clothes/Women are always playing hard to get/No man likes an easy woman/Women should be struck regularly, like gongs/Women like to be raped/Women are always crying about something/Women don't understand the value of a dollar/ . . . /Don't worry your pretty little head about it/Dumb broad/It is glorious to be the mother of all mankind/A woman's work is never done/All you do is cook and clean and sit around all day/Women are only interested in trapping some man/A woman who can't hold a man isn't much of a

45

woman/Women hate to be with other women/Women are always off chattering with each other/Some of my best friends are women. . . ."[5]

Woman-child in the promised land!

The answer in the women's liberation movement of how the girl becomes a woman is:

> When she defines her own life and stops being controlled by her family, her boyfriend, or her boss. When she learns to stand up and fight for herself and other women—because she has learned that her problems aren't just her own.
> *All over the world, girls are growing up. . . .*

For the sake of a framework to which we can refer and from which we can generalize, let me remind you of an encounter of Jesus with two women.

He stops at the home of his friends (Luke 10:38-42, JB). Mary drops what she's doing in order to be with him. Martha, on the other hand, bustles about with preparations. She is so preoccupied with taking care of things she is unable to be with him. She even interrupts what's going on to complain:

"Lord, don't you care that my sister is leaving me to do the serving all by myself? Please tell her to help me."

"Martha," he responds, "Martha, you worry and fret about so many things, and yet few are needed, indeed, only one. It is Mary who has chosen the good part; it is not to be taken from her."

Martha symbolizes so much of the old me for women. She gives too much of herself and gets too little for herself in return. She concentrates on menus and manners and meals. She misses the meaning of human presence.

Mary, on the other hand, symbolizes much of a new i for women. She puts aside the drudgery of duty for the delight of relationship. She expresses what she wants rather than doing what others demand. The good part is allowing the material—that is, the survival needs of food, clothes, and shelter—to be put aside and the spiritual—that is, the identity needs for closeness, caring, and recognition—to be expressed.

While Jesus commends Mary, he does not dismiss Martha. Mary's responsive spontaneity—being with him—goes along with, and in part depends upon, Martha's responsible structure—

46

preparing the place. Disproportionately, however, the trustworthy Martha limits the setting in which she functions reliably. She becomes martyr to the deadliness of routine whether at home or in the office.

At the level of survival—keeping life and limb together—a woman knows who she is.

A Chicano woman put it precisely: "When your race is fighting for survival—to eat, to be clothed, to be housed, to be left in peace—as a woman, you know who you are. You are the principle of life, of survival and endurance." [6] Thus, women of every group struggling simply to exist carry the burden of being.

Lower middle-class women, therefore, are not caught in the home. Rather they are trapped in the womb of the world. They have to get out and work in order to help house and feed and clothe their families.

Women who must work (as well as women who choose to work) invariably come out on the lower rung of the recognition ladder. Consider male/female discrepancies for full-time year-round median income in the 1970 and 1971 census figures, respectively:[7]

	1970	1971
Professionals & Technicians		
male	$12,477	$12,842
female	8,005	8,515
Managers, Administrators		
male	9,765	11,292
female	4,616	5,523
Clerical Workers		
male	7,034	7,965
female	4,002	4,646
Sales Workers		
male	7,367	8,321
female	2,248	2,279

The full-time income in these years for all workers only reinforces the discrepancies:

	1970	1971
white males	$9,709	$9,902
nonwhite males	6,638	7,006
white females	5,536	5,767
nonwhite females	4,664	5,194

As these income statistics reveal, there is a greater difference between the incomes of men and women than between white and black. If income levels reveal anything at all about the values of a society, we can see the problem faced by women as they try to break through to what it means to be persons in their own right. They are trapped in the role of Martha, the old me, the drudgery of duty.

It is the black and brown women who represent that bondage of the old me most acutely. For "the 'job' of the upper-class woman to 'supervise' . . . menu-planning, endless shopping, genteel hostess routine . . . is just a diamond-studded variation of the usual female role."[8] So black women have been described as "slave of a slave" double jeopardy: black and female. We "have always been told by black men," declares the Black Women's Liberation Group, "that we were black, ugly, evil bitches and whores—in other words we were the real niggers in this society—oppressed by whites, male and female, and the black man, too."[9]

Middle- and upper-class women, however, who have provided much of the passion and power for women's liberation, have not been caught only in the world. They are also trapped in the womb of the home. They stay home and work in order to help their husbands succeed and their children grow up.

That Chicano woman spoke of the contrast: "For the young, alienated Anglos, on the other hand, the family as it has functioned in the past often reflects a bundle of false values in a lying society of which she is part. Her position is almost the opposite of the Chicana's."[10]

Another Mexican American woman spells out the tragic implications of a woman's subordinating her life to that of her husband and children. The wife/mother seems to become more domineering and demanding as he and they grow more successful. This is the price, as she puts it, of owning a slave:

> A woman who has no way of expressing herself and of realizing herself as a full human has nothing else to turn to but the owning of material things. She builds her entire life around these, and finds security in this way. All she has to live for is her house and family; she becomes very possessive of both. This makes her a totally dependent human.[11]

48

Whether trapped in the tomb of the home or caught in the tomb of the world (of work), women know their place! Their place has been serving others: children and men first, and men first of all. St. Thomas Aquinas was asked if the image of God is found in every person: "Yes, it is," he answered, "but this does not apply to woman, since she was made in the image of man, not God. . . ." [12] Women have been niggers!

In a multitude of ways the Marys of the world are rebelling. They reject the nigger image; they demand the human image. The old me of the regulated routine does not fit. A new i of the spontaneous and responsive asserts itself. To grow as a woman inevitably means acquiring new goals, new recognition, new relationships, new involvements, new significance.

However, the issue is not as simple as giving up the regulated routine of Martha for the spontaneous responsiveness of Mary. In seeing the limitation of the conventional we can too easily overlook the limitation of the unconventional. To learn that one pattern never can be everything, we need to remember that each pattern contributes something necessary to the whole.

Let's look at this search for an i as a woman through the experience of one woman. I propose we do so by considering several of her dreams.

Dreams, by virtue of their symbolic nature and their freedom from the testing of space and time, touch the most deeply personal parts of ourselves and so tap the most universal resources of our lives. While a dream expresses our own individuality, it also reflects our universal humanity. With and in the dream we express and explore that which we have neglected or rejected in our waking state. [13]

In biblical and post-biblical times people took dreams to be manifestations of the holy. They were revelations of and by and from God. Equally, dreams have played a prominent role in the arts and sciences. They disclose the hidden creative and inspirational potential in human beings. [14]

The dream may be regarded as the voice of that centeredness within us that works on our becoming whole. In it we see the old me and a new i struggling with each other for a more fully *human* being. It allows us to show who we are in a profound way, to say something about our way of life and our concept of ourselves. It is our own message to ourselves about our being and becoming ourselves.

49

Think of the dream as a moving picture-puzzle. As a visual image, the dream presents instantaneously a great amount of personally relevant material. Even more than a picture, though, the dream is a drama. The dreamer herself or himself is the writer, the players, the scenery, the props, the animals, the objects, and the audience simultaneously and separately. Through the pictorial drama, the dream projects the inner world into a semi-outer world. Every aspect represents some aspect of the dreamer's self and world.

Now, what do I need to tell you about this woman in order for you to understand her dreams? I call her Joan to emphasize her being a person while not identifying her personally.

Joan is: white, thirty years of age, a minister, married to a minister, obviously well-educated. Her struggle to be(come) a new i is not a matter of sickness but of health, not a process of simply expressing her feelings but of genuinely finding her self, not a private affair of inadequacy but a universal quest for humanization. But let her dreams speak on her *and* our behalf.

Joan's first dream sets out the growing i inside:

> I have discovered an underground passage. It seems that others know the passage is there, but I find some new section of it or something. An older woman is to go with me.

The inner life invariably has been portrayed as underground. It is the ground out of which life springs, the source in which life roots, the place of our beginning, and the place of our ending. Seldom do we enter it alone. Usually we are accompanied by a guide—sometimes a man, more often a woman.

The older woman, according to Joan, is a person with whom both she and her husband associate. Joan's husband feels very negative toward her because of the woman's supposed rigidity. Joan's own feelings toward her are negative, but mostly they reflect her husband's feelings.

Joan continues:

> Both of us are excited about discovering where the passage will lead. I feel it will lead to some "very old treasure"; but I am uncertain about this. The entrance to the passage is in our basement. Even though it isn't the house we live in, it is "our" house and familiar. The woman and I do not want anyone to know about the passage.
>
> There are some workmen in the house working right where we have to pass by. They are sitting and kneeling on the floor around their tools and work. We decide not to risk the secrecy of the passage so we are not able to go while they are there.

The older woman goes home. Shortly afterwards the workmen begin to gather their tools to go out for lunch. She comes back. We feel an urgency to get going because they will return soon and we will have missed our chance.

As we begin approaching the entrance, the surrounding area is very dimly lit. I realize that the passage itself is pitch black. She is leading the way, and I ask if she has a flashlight. She says, of course she does. She has been holding it in a way that concealed it from me.

I stop again and say I think it would be a good idea if I take along some paper and a pencil to keep track of the way we go so we will not get lost and can get there again. She approves of this plan.

We set out together, but later on I am on my own. The impression I get is that she has been "called away."

We know what we expect to find and are pleased about it. There are keys involved and many choices regarding doors into the passages and the turns we can take. The doors to the passage are heavy wood but short and have large metal rings as handles. The ways out of the passages—which seem to come up in the homes of various people around the community—are seemingly "doorless." It is like I will kind of "pop right out."

At one point I come up in the apartment of a black family. I have "gone to school" with the man. It is OK that I am there in spite of the fact they haven't expected me. The wife offers me something to eat. I have very positive feelings about her.

At another point I emerge absolutely nude. In order to get where I want in the passages, it has been necessary to go that way (perhaps in the last stages). I feel very matter-of-fact about it because it is necessary. I am sure about that even when others are startled I came out that way.

That so much material appeared in this dream suggests the complexity and yet-to-be-realized-centeredness of Joan's struggle to be an i. How can we get a handle on understanding it? Since a dreamer's own reflections are usually the most accurate clues to the meanings of a dream, I encouraged Joan to suggest what it meant to her.

She saw the underground passages as her inner self which she is seeking to come to terms with, to understand, and to make more fully a part of her self. The darkness and the going into the depth signified journeying into her own depths. She experienced a real feeling of cooperation and friendliness and trust between the woman and herself. The older woman—and she had been rejecting such women—had something to offer her in her exploration: providing light in order to see and leading the way at the beginning. Martha was not all bad.

After the dream Joan's feelings about the older woman grew significantly warmer. She felt that what the woman represented— perhaps even the rigidity—had something to offer her. Clearly, it is something in herself from which she can benefit in her explorations, even though she has to do them for the most part on her own. What she is searching for is something somehow familiar, old and valuable: the truly and fully human image of herself.

Joan had to seize the chance to get into the passage when the opportunity arose. Those "hard working men" at the entrance had to take a break. Part of herself, she saw, stands in the way of making the journey. And that part comes through as masculine, since men and tools both conveyed that to her. But she could not do anything to make the men leave. Perhaps, she thought, the time "has to be ripe."

The older woman is a feminine symbol to Joan. It told her that "working with" what the woman symbolized in her is the way to get at the treasure. Her wanting paper and pencil is her effort to keep track of the way she has traveled.

Some people claim that a black person in dreams symbolizes the "dark" and "hidden" aspects of oneself. Here the black woman is friendly and helpful. Joan felt that part to be another step toward her acceptance of the contrasts within herself. Perhaps, she thought, the "dark" side will have something to "feed" me at some point.

She saw the round metal handles on the doors as symbols of the doors leading to wholeness, unity within herself and union with others. Even though the doors were heavy, they, too, seemed more friendly than threatening. The passages, although underground, were not cold but only old and dark. The choices as to directions spoke to her of decisions she is responsible for making in her own becoming. Since the passages opened into various homes, she saw herself emerging in a variety of settings. But everything spread out from the central passage. "There is a unity," she affirmed, "about the core from which I operate."

Despite her usual negative feelings about her body and others "seeing" it, her coming out nude said something to her about her ability to be open about who she was. She could accept herself and let others see her as she was.

During this period she chose to be in a position that tested her emerging i. She entered that situation with an increased confidence to make better use of her abilities. Then, horror of horrors: she failed to respond! All the opposite poles of where she felt she had been growing emerged: low self-esteem, inability to assess herself accurately, inability to make use of her knowledge and skills, and a narrowing of her ability to see. All of that "old stuff"—the old me—overtook her.

A dream in three very clear sections followed shortly afterward. It symbolizes her struggle and suggests what she must do to be an i:

> *I am driving my car very fast through a dingy part of a city. I am annoyed because I am held back by the traffic. It is all moving in the same direction, but it is going too slowly for my hurry. It keeps stopping so that I have to slam on the brakes.*
>
> *Finally, I break out of the traffic. The road ahead is clear. I drive even faster. I come to a high bridge which curves sharply to the left and to the right. The car goes out of control; it slides along the railing of the bridge. The railings open up, and the car slips through. But I am left on the bridge watching it fall:*

Joan portrays her problem as rushing. She had been in a hurry to get out of the city (her situation) where she was driving. She also was hurrying *to* something (a fuller self). Now she is faced with the problem of not being able to get there. She has *lost* her car, her way of getting around, her selfhood.

> *In the second segment, I leave my car in a parking lot and walk through an unfamiliar city to meet Henry [her husband] at a restaurant. I try to make a point of noting landmarks so I can find the car, but I am involved in getting where I am going.*
>
> *The moment the meal is served, I get up and leave. I feel I have to find my car. I think I can do it quickly.*
>
> *I find the area unfamiliar. It takes a long time. I never go back to my meal, which, by the way, is one of my favorites.*
>
> *In the third segment, I am held captive along with a group of people I am with. I have left my car behind, not wanting to take it on the island where we are later held prisoners. I realize it is my car that could get us out of our predicament, not only myself but the others as well. But I have left it behind and can't get back to it. Some of the others are able to get back to the car "for me."*

Joan's car is important to her. It has been a good car, and she has had it for six years. Never had she dreamed about it before. In this one night, though, it is lost three different times and needed three different times when she does not have it. Her sense of i-ness is in serious trouble.

53

The first time she sees herself in such a hurry to get away from where she is—leave behind some old patterns—and to get somewhere else that she ends up losing that which can help her get there. The second time she fails to learn the route by which she traveled. Her rushing to find her way again results in leaving behind something she wants and would enjoy. The third time she finds that she may need what she leaves behind, for herself and maybe for others as well. She realizes she is cut off from something she needs.

Joan's tendency is to want to leave behind that of herself which she has experienced as negative. She does not want it; she does not need it; if she could just put some distance between it and herself, she would be safe. But, as she told herself through her dreams, "This isn't true!"

In becoming oneself one must take in through acceptance and assimilation what has gone before. One must *own one's past as one's own.* When one rejects fragments of what has gone into the making of oneself, one fails to "hang together." One experiences oneself in pieces—one's several selves.

Joan's dreams seem to be telling her she needs to slow down. She must assimilate the route by which she has come. She has to take with her that which at times seems to be more of a burden than a blessing. Martha cannot be forgotten.

Joan's dreams seem to be telling her she can lose out if she throws out the old me, for it is her "me" that aids her search for the "old" i. What has been a part of her turns out to be helpful. Growth means taking the old along with her, even while she moves beyond that "me."

Joan came away from her failure to respond and from her searching for a new i with an increased sense that any experience is what she makes of it. Even ends, she saw, have openness about them, as in the resurrection. At one time the "failure" would have meant an end for her. Now she felt more able to use it by making of it a new beginning. From her old me came a new i.

There is one further dream that helps us see the process of becoming a new i as a woman. It lights up the necessity of routine responsiveness and a responsive routine. Both the Martha and the Mary sides of her personality must be developed. It equally suggests a going beyond the rigidness implied in *the* old me and the casualness implicit in *a* new i. To understand the dream, you need to know that Joan's hobby is sculpturing. Most of her figures have been faceless and sexually ambiguous. Recently she has done some clearly feminine heads, yet she continues to choose to leave some parts rough and undefined.

I am once more in a big hurry. I am expected to help prepare for some ceremony, perhaps a wedding. I am supposed to have clay figures of Mary and Joseph ready.

I am late. I rush into the room where everyone is waiting and look at Joseph. He is ready. I set him aside.

Then I realize I have left Mary unfinished. I seem to say to myself, "I did't MEAN to leave her that way!" Her head and face are pretty well finished and clearly defined, but the rest of her is undefined. There is a lot of work yet to do on her before she is finished. I feel pretty desperate because I have to be ready so soon.

I work at it—taking some clay off one side and putting her down. She falls over. So I put some clay back in a different way. I do the same thing with the other side. When she falls over, I am afraid she will smash her head. The clay is very soft.

There are lots of people around, but I don't even consider asking anyone for help. I wouldn't expect them to be able to do anything to help. Then my father comes in and looks at me. I think that he is the one person I can trust to help me work on it, for he is artistic and very skilled with his hands. But I don't ask him, and the dream just goes on.

Mary is very necessary for what is going to take place. I know this very clearly.

This dream continues the process of Joan's working out her i as a woman. She has been very aware of how she experiences the act of creating a sculpture. It is slow and somehow born out of her and out of itself. It has an independent way of becoming itself. There is a lot of letting it evolve for itself. The material itself sometimes "tells" her what "it wants to become."

The dream moves her understanding of this process of creating to the process of creating herself—a new i as a woman. It says, as does the previous dream, slow down. It also says, as in the experience of creating a sculpture, you can't know what the outcome will be. You have to do some testing and trying-out; you have to remove one piece, replace some part, reshape, rearrange, and in each case find what makes the whole "become," without really being sure ahead of time what it will be.

Her father's appearance appears to be saying that the masculine can be helpful in shaping the feminine. But there seems to be some way in which she is refusing to let it help by not asking anything of it. Joseph's being finished provides a clear reference to her more developed masculine part. After having decided to leave Mary—the feminine part of her—the way she was, she now feels dissatisfied. In fact, she wants to do more work on her feminine aspects. While her head—her thinking—is finished, now she needs to work on the

55

rest—her sexuality and her feelings. Previously, her grasp on her identity has not developed much beyond the head.

Joan finds herself wondering what her next work of sculpture—really her next work of selfhood—will express. She feels funny in knowing that it will be something which she will do herself, and yet she is eager to know what it will be since she can *not know* in advance. What exciting possibilities!

Germaine Greer wrote *The Female Eunuch* with the hope that "women will discover that they have a will." [15]

Under the tyranny of the old me—the woman-child—women still have a will, but it is an inverted, distorted, and deceptive will. It makes demands upon the environment to act on its behalf: "Don't you care . . . ?" "After all I've done for you. . . ." "Why don't you tell them to. . . ."

In Martha, we can sense the old me of a girl who becomes such a woman-child. Her good intentions erode under the pressures of carrying them out. She gives her life away in duty to others by denying her duty to herself. Whether she denies her self deliberately or unintentionally, the result is the same: the loss of joy in living. What begins as delightful sharing changes into a deadly chore. What grows out of genuine commitment turns into strained duress. Instead of investing herself in the present, she has an investment in the past and the future. A living relationship hardens into a routine affair.

Women as a group tend to center their feelings, their enjoyment, and their ambition in something outside of themselves. [16] They want to serve and to share. They disclose more of a harmony between themselves and the world than men do. But when a woman's will is centered only in a home and family—because that's the way it should be; when a woman's only significant contribution is the success of her husband and her children—because that's her duty; when a woman's chief expression of creativity and life's work is keeping the household schedule running smoothly—because that's her role—then she, her husband, her children, her neighbors, her friends, and the entire community all suffer for it!

In Mary, we see a new i of a girl who becomes a woman. She rejects the routine and the conventional for the sake of spontaneity and surprise. She expresses "her" desire for a relationship *by* relating. And it is her spontaneous relating that calls forth Jesus' recognition and confirmation.

Martha continues as a role, a function, a servant. In neglecting herself she cuts off a relationship. Mary, in contrast, expresses herself as a person, a participant, a presence. In expressing herself she enters into a relationship.

We see in Joan that womanly will asserting itself. It means letting go of the routine of the everyday as an end in itself. It means drawing upon that regulating will to look for more than meets the eye. It means shifting from what is expected to what is unexpected. It means seeking for and being nourished by the hidden and rejected feminine parts of herself. It means bursting out—in many places, in full view—as she is.

In order to come out as herself, Joan has to go into herself. She has to give up the security of an exaggerated masculine mastery for the sake of the creativity of an unfinished feminine warmth. Instead of a limited sphere she must now meet people in many spheres. Her involvements have to be finding places outside of herself and her home for entering and centering.

Even under conditions of having to work for survival rather than identity, there is liberation in serving in spheres away from home.

Doris is the wife of a lower-class middle American, one of the many interviewed by Robert Coles. She has four children to care for, a house to keep *very* clean, an aged mother to visit, and lately she has had to find work. She helps out in a luncheonette two hours at noon five days a week. Her husband does not like her working, but she got her way.

What Doris likes about serving the crowded tables is "a view of the outside world. She meets people. She hears people talk, and she learns what is on their minds." [17] With the few dollars she makes she feels more independent. Time passes quickly. Despite her dislike of all the talk about the problems of the world, she finds herself listening intently to what others are saying. She brings more to her relationships at home.

That sense of independence—of being someone in one's own right; of expressing what one wants with the same legitimacy as all others declaring what they want; of risking the give-and-take of being out in the open; of experiencing the excitement of being on the road; of letting evolve what cannot be reduced to simple routine; of asserting oneself by expressing oneself—here is the joy of being a woman with an i.

But a woman's will must never mean adopting masculine aggressiveness, for there is danger in "driving" hurriedly through the world. There is blindness in neglecting to note one's surroundings. There is foolishness in leaving behind one's strengths.

Joan found she needed her old patterns of the routine to get her started on exploring who she was. She had to depend on both her feminine and her masculine qualities in becoming a full *human* being. Recognition comes through her relationships and her responsibilities, not through her self-sufficiency. To assert what she wants, finally, means giving of herself in creative expression.

To be a woman is to invest oneself in self-chosen activity.

To be a woman is to feel pride and confidence in trying this and experimenting with that.

To be a woman is to communicate and to cooperate with a variety of people based on the delight of companionship and the diligence in shared endeavors.

To be a woman is to have
    something to desire
    something to make
    something to achieve
and ultimately,
    something to give.
That is the *human* image of a woman!

So, one woman can write "For Witches" or, more accurately, for what I am contending, namely, women with will:

    today i began
    to find
    myself.

    tomorrow
    perhaps
    i will begin
    to find
    you.[18]

FOUR

To Be An i—As A Man

How does a boy become a man?

Thus, the question of a new i can be asked by men's liberation. It implies the backdrop of the old me of how a boy becomes a guy: blue and simple clothes, cars and collisions, noise and roughhousing—he's lusty and lusting, daring and aggressive. And—

> A man's place is in the world/Men are such exciting people/Men's talk is real talk/Intelligent men are the best leaders/It's a man's duty to work/Men are the breadwinners/Men don't cry/Men are reasonable and realistic/Men are tough/A man has a right to be left alone/Men know the value of money/A man doesn't think about clothes/Men like to be the center of things/Men need to be with the boys/Men like to run around and play it fast and loose/Men have it made. . . .

Man-child in the promised land!

59

The answer in the men's liberation movement of how the boy becomes a man would be:

> When he defines his own life and stops being controlled by his

aggressive desires and his achievement needs. When he learns to love and to care for himself and for others—because he has learned that his problems aren't just his own.
All over the world, boys are growing up. . . .

A male graduate student of mine once turned in a reaction paper on several readings organized around the theme of knowing and becoming oneself.

He began with a quotation from Genesis (4:9,JB) that underscored a demanding question by God and a defensive question from man: "Where is your brother Abel? . . . Am I my brother's guardian?" With these biblical references the student had pointed to the old me of the male: namely, too much will and not enough love, too much self and not enough other.

While the student's reference to "man" meant mankind, we can read it as dealing with men and their predicament. The student went on to write:

Indeed, you are your brother's keeper! You are responsible for your fellowman; you are responsible for your own self. These themes run through the various writings, and all relate to the general thesis that man is not man. He is a manipulator; he is a technocrat; he is determined by his environment, responding only to input or stimuli; he is a completely free agent; he is a hyprocrite; he is a snake worshiper shifting responsibility to others; he is not human.

That student developed these issues with cogency and sophistication. The reader would get little sense of where he was in terms of his own humanness even though he wrote of humanness. Then came the final paragraph:

. . . I long was tormented by the conflict between what people told me I should do, and what I wanted to do. Not that I was certain of what I wanted to do or be, but I wanted to be the one to find out for myself.

I want to search on my own, not alone, but with others who are searching, too. Through them I can see myself to some extent. I can help others in a like manner.

I made little or no progress toward this end until I realized just what my condition was. And the price was great! My sister killed herself after I tried to help. I discovered I hardly knew her or myself.

A man is real if he is living the truth of his life. Then his reality awakens life in others. A man is dead if he lives against the truth of his life. Then his deadness kills life in others.

In order not to die and in order not to kill, men need to discover who they are. To discover who they are requires their knowing what they really care about and living the truth of that care.

Yet men, particularly, are afraid to discover who they are.[1] They take little time to look and to listen. They drive themselves at work. They shield themselves at home. They feel tough when they act childish. They compete and they control. They exclude and they dominate. They play their cards close to their vests. The male role—

> don't let others know you
> don't let others see you
> keep your relationships impersonal
>   and objective
> hide your real self
> don't acknowledge or express the breadth
>   and depth of your inner feelings—

has lethal consequences:

> —a chronic burden of stress
> —excessive energy expended in
>   keeping spontaneous inner
>   experience to one's self
> —a shorter life span
> —greater health hazards
> —less insight into self
> —less understanding of others
> —incompetence at loving
> —difficulty in receiving love.

61

The real questions for man—black or white, white collar or blue collar or professional, middle or marginal--are: "Who am I? What sort of culture should I have, what is my heritage, what should my pride be?"[2]

A parable Jesus told of two boys (Luke 15:11-32) provides a framework to which we can refer and from which we can generalize on male bondage and male liberation. Whereas the framework of Martha and Mary came directly from real people, this one only reflects real people. To that extent the two patterns are not parallel. Yet the parable does aid us in looking at male bondage.

In the parable one son finds himself; the other does not. One breaks loose and grows up by getting himself together; the other stays tight and remains childish by keeping his life apart. One becomes a man; the other continues a boy.

These life-styles contrast the freedom of a man to become who he is and the constriction of one remaining only a role. How, we are asking, can men live the truth of their individuality? How can men deal with their need to be themselves and their fear of being themselves? How can men respond to their desire to be part of the life of others and their resistance to that sharing? What do these life-styles suggest?

Now in using the parable as a way of looking at men finding who they are and growing up, I remind you that Jesus told the parable to make a different point. He was stressing God's constant care, not men becoming genuinely human. He emphasized the waiting Father instead of the aggressive Dad. In making that point, however, Jesus was showing the loss of life in separation and isolation. He was calling for the recovery of life through reunion and responsiveness. The loss of the likeness of the divine image is recovered in the lived reality of a human image.

The older brother symbolizes so much of the old me for men. He shares too little of himself in what he does. He wants too much for himself in return for what he does. He is a mystery to those around him. He remains a puzzle to the i within.

The older brother of this world gives every appearance of being establishment. He exhibits extreme cautiousness. He stays home and cares for the organization. He keeps things going. He conserves the community's values. He hangs on and stays with it. He acts responsibly.

This cautiousness leads to a certain calculation on his part. At the public level of observable behavior, he maintains the family and the family business. At the private level of intentions and desires, he (later) reveals he acts primarily to maintain himself and to get his "goodies." Behind the mask of responsibility we glimpse the face of willfulness. We can never be quite certain where he is and what he is doing.

For instance, how does he react when the brother who rejected the male role comes home? He complains: "Look at all these years I have gone to work, followed what was expected. I never broke a law or disobeyed an order. Yet I never got any recognition, never so much as a little party, let alone a big blast."

The men who play the responsible male role feel cheated. They miss out on things they want. A fracture splits the way they seem on the outside from the way they feel on the inside.

Such a split between acting and feeling makes for escalating deception. His actions disguise his intentions. Every response requires calculation: how will this look? what will others think? dare I risk exposure? He brings a hidden agenda to every situation. What he says fails to disclose what he experiences.

Thus, men convey an air of detached objectivity. There is a real sense in which they are never quite "with" what they're doing. They go through motions without experiencing or expressing the emotions we normally expect to accompany behavior. They are simply not there, and one is left wondering what it is they really want.

In an ironic twist, the dominant older son ends up being a dominated little boy. He is always scanning the environment to see what's what. He is ever dependent upon others to determine what he does and who he is. Somehow he never experiences himself as a necessary part of what happens.

Recall his complaint again: "Look at all the years I have slaved for you! I never disobeyed a single order, and yet you have never given me...." He blames his unhappiness on circumstances—the father's insensitivity to how "good" he was, the unrewarded thankless job at which he slaved, the permissiveness shown to the deviant. It is not he but his world that's at fault.

At no point in the parable do I sense he feels himself to be a source of decision and action. Authority and initiative lie elsewhere. He experiences himself pushed around by the whims and wishes of others. Feeling like an object, he treats himself like an object. If hungry, he would complain, "My stomach is hungry," as though his stomach were not part of him.

The "good" man has little "say" over his life. He is a pawn in someone else's chess game.

There comes a loss of reality in this work-dominating pattern. A man's main activity fails to express who he is. He defers—perhaps eventually even abandons—"his real needs," as Charles Reich informs us, in *The Greening of America*, "and increasingly his wants [become] subject to outside manipulation. Losing both his work-essence and his need-essence, man [is] no longer a unique individual but an extension of the production-consumption system." [3] He wears himself out pursuing an identity that is not his own.

The male goals of recognition and accomplishment, of power and possessions, are not merely wrong. "They are," contends Reich, *"unreal.* A person whose life is one long ego trip or power trip has not merely chosen one kind of satisfaction in preference to others; he has chosen goals that have no real relationship to personal growth, satisfaction, or happiness." [4]

No wonder the older boy feels hurt and bitter and resentful. Life has passed him by. He has been cheated out of his recognition and his enjoyment. He has been denied the benefits of the system's generosity. And he is not to blame. The boss and the no-goods and the freeloaders and the radicals and the long-hairs and the system have failed. What is right does not pay off. The world is the source of his unhappiness, not himself.

In contrast, the younger boy symbolizes the possibility of a new i for men. He expresses what he wants. He acts on what he thinks. There's nothing cautious about him. He is carefree, almost to the point of irresponsibility.

He wants to leave home, and he does. He rejects the organization and heads for the city. He makes eyebrows rise, heads turn, tongues wag. He has no concern for the values others care about. He is out for meaning and to heck with the means.

Yet, despite his flaunting of convention, there is an engaging honesty about him. While concerned only with himself, he lets others know where he is. He levels about his wants: "Give me my share of the goods," and off he goes. There is no calculation, no deception, no disguise. His intent is perfectly clear—get away from home, bum around, seek the thrills, forget the headaches, have instant salvation, take what I want when I want it—now!

No matter how we may feel about the pattern, there is a

transparency in such self-disclosure. His actions show who he is. His responses are clear messages. Whether one likes it or not, one knows where he's at.

There is a sense in which he participates in what he does without reservation. When he leaves, others know he is leaving. When he returns, others know he has returned. He does what he is doing when he is doing it. He is wholly there, with it, without phoniness, without pretense.

In an ironic twist, the irresponsible boy turns out to be a responsible man. He answers for himself. He lives as though decisions and actions depend upon him and no one else. He takes responsibility for what happens. Hear his conclusion: "I left home. I sinned. I failed." He shoulders the blame. He assumes the guilt. He stops the excuses.

Notice the pronouns he uses. They are all first person singular— I, me, mine. Recall the pronouns the older boy used. They are second and third person—you, he, him. At every point the young man experiences himself as the source of what happens. Initiative lies with him. He determines what he does. He accepts the consequences.

When the dropout leaves home, it is not because of the overbearing arrogance of the square but because he chooses to go. When the turned-off is taken by the big city, it is not because of the hustlers but because he lets himself be taken. When the homeless hippy is reduced to nothing, it is not because of hard times and hard hats but because he lets himself get to nothing. When he becomes hungry, he does not treat his stomach as though it were not a part of him but can say, "*I* perish with hunger." The young man has "say" over his life.

Although subtle, the contrast between the old me of the male role and an i as a man is sharp. At any particular moment the difference might not be apparent. Over a span of time the pattern grows clear.

While appearing very responsible, the older boy actually takes no responsibility for what happens. He passes the buck. He "leaves it to the snake." His sin is passivity, apathy, acedia, doing too little and expecting too much. Despite his surface aggression, he hides his inner emptiness. He turns himself into a pawn by seeing what he does as not coming from himself but rather forced upon him from the outside. So he rightly feels bitter.

While appearing very irresponsible, the young man actually

assumes responsibility for what happens. The buck stops with him. His sin is activity, assertiveness, hubris, overconfidence, doing a lot and settling for a little. He experiences himself as a person by seeing what he does as coming from and determined by himself. So he rightly experiences guilt.

The clue to the difference between the lethal aspects of the old male role and the living aspects of a new male i lies embedded in the intriguing phrase in the parable, "And he came to his senses." It can be translated: he came to himself; he woke up; he saw who he was; he experienced what was happening; he became aware.

Awareness bears some crucial connection with our becoming who we are. Again and again the Bible refers to those who have eyes yet are blind, those who have ears yet are deaf, those who have hearts yet do not feel. They are unaware—insensitive—to the truth of their situation.

The older boy never sensed what was there. He wanted to be appreciated. He failed to see his father's constant appreciation. "My son, you and I are always together; all I have is yours." He wanted to have a blast—to play and sing and dance. He failed to see how he kept himself from joining the party. He tied himself up in knots: fists clenched, jaws tight, muscles tensed, head throbbing, heart pounding. Without knowing it, he held himself back. Without seeing it, he kept himself shut off. Without intending it, he killed his own liveliness.

The man who submits to this culture, according to Alan Watts, is "almost literally, a zombie. He is docile and 'mature' in the style of our drab and dismal bourgeoisie; he is quite incapable of gaiety or exuberance; he believes he is dancing when he is shuffling around a room. . . ."[5]

Because men play a part, they miss what they want. Because they put up a front, they lose touch with themselves. Because they fool others, they end up deceiving themselves. Literally, they become blind to what goes on. They are incapable of seeing the obvious. As Ephesians (4:18) describes such a condition, they live blindfolded in a world of illusion, cut off from the life of God through ignorance and insensitivity.

In response to my urging an honest acceptance and open expression of who one is and what one wants, an establishment executive—visibly shaken at the thought—claimed my point of view to be "very dangerous." "If I had only what you said to go on," he warned, "I would go out and sow my wild oats." The very denial of his needs and the very threat of their expression reveal the depth of his alienation from himself.

More in touch with the truth is the response of a thirty-year-old mother of three elementary age children: "It's sort of scary to think of going off and just being yourself." She acknowledges her pattern of putting her self aside. She experiences the dizzy possibilities of letting her i out. She prepares the way for getting the old me and a new i together.

It has become increasingly obvious that men's identity and their self-esteem have rested on too narrow a base. Although women have been caught in the home, now we are seeing that men are caught in the world. "If men can see themselves as manly, and life as worth-while, only as long as they are engaged in gainful employ, or are sexually potent, or have enviable social status, then clearly these are tenuous bases upon which to ground one's existence." [6] To be locked into the old me of the male role is to be lost to life.

In contrast, the younger man eventually woke up to what was happening. He came to his senses. He opened his eyes. He heard with his ears. He felt with his heart. He found what he wanted. He realized that what he thought he wanted—fun and freedom without responsibility—were not what he wanted at all. What mattered to him was being with those he cared about, belonging to a family, carrying his share of being part of the human community. His fantasies of freedom turned out to be actual slavery. His fearfulness of responsibility took on the direction of liberation.

In *Nobody Knows My Name,* black author James Baldwin describes the disillusionment of the American writer who flees to Europe to escape America. Baldwin, of course, is speaking autobiographically:

> This is a personal day, a terrible day, the day to which his entire sojourn has been tending. It is the day he realizes that there are no untroubled countries in this fearfully troubled world; that if he has been preparing himself for anything in Europe, he has been preparing himself—for America. In short, the freedom that the American writer finds in Europe brings him, full circle, back to himself, with the responsibility for his development where it always was: in his own hands.[7]

In other words, what happens to one does not add up to what one expects and wants to happen. So, the younger son, Baldwin, the American writer abroad, the dropout, the seeker after greener pastures, looks around to see what is wrong. He senses where he is—not so much physically as psychologically, spiritually, personally, humanly, pilgrimage-wise. He knows what he is and is not experiencing. He begins to see more clearly what does and does not matter to him. He becomes aware of the truth of his situation.

"How many hired men of my father's have more than enough to eat, and here I am dying of hunger! I will get up and go back to my father, and I will say to him, 'Father, I have done wrong in the sight of Heaven and in your eyes. I do not deserve to be called your son anymore. Please take me on as one of your hired men.'"

For the first time the *now* young *man* woke up to what was taking place. He saw *his* own actions in terms of their impact. He experienced the consequences of *his* behavior. Because he had acted as he felt, he could discover what he wanted. Because he had expressed who he was, he could get in touch with where he was. Because he had not fooled others, he could not kid himself. Literally, he opened his eyes and saw. He came to his senses. His senses came to him. His senses made sense!

In the old me of the male role, men's actions and men's attitudes turn out to be irresponsibly responsible. Such men appear together on the outside, yet are lonely on the inside. Because they seldom act as they feel and because they shift initiative to others, such men grow less and less aware of the truth of their situation.

In a new i as a man, men's actions and men's attitudes end up being responsibly irresponsible. Such men create havoc on the outside and come together on the inside. Because they act as they feel and because they take initiative for what happens, such men grow more and more aware of what matters to them.

How unfortunate and tragic that men allow themselves to become locked into such separate and competitive roles. Either be "good" and "respectable" or "bad" and "disreputable." Neither staying home nor taking off is a satisfactory answer. Where one lives matters less; how one lives matters more.

Perhaps the decisive difference between becoming who one is and losing who one is grows out of the way each son responded to anxiety.

Anxiety represents the gap between the known and the unknown. When uncomfortable, we are tempted to hang on to the safe and the secure and the familiar. Yet another part of us pushes to move into the uncertain and the insecure and the unknown. In that constricted narrow passage between pulling back or plunging ahead, we experience our whole life on the line. The threat is total threat: I am something or I am nothing; I am or I am not; you care or you don't.

What did the older boy do when upset? How did he deal with threat?

He avoided the situation. He stayed away from the house. He asked the servants what was what. He demanded that his father come out to him. He covered up his anxiety with anger and irritation and threats and accusation and bitterness. He reacted with self-righteous indignation. He exhibited infantile behavior. He shut himself out.

When the old me of the male role feels uncomfortable, one pulls back. Consequently, one never experiences the liberation that comes from moving into and through and out from the valley of dread. Women remain bitches; competitors bastards; blacks niggers; whites honkies; liberals weirdos; men chauvinist pigs; conservatives diehards. Differences deepen threat and escalate destruction.

Invectives mask impotence. The louder they scream, the more helpless they feel. The tougher they act, the weaker they are.

What did the young man do when upset? How did he deal with threat?

Eventually he moved into it. He stayed with it. He met uncomfortableness head on "I will get up and go back to my father. . . ." He experienced the loss of relationship for what it was. He owned up to the loss of self-respect for what it was. He took the consequences for what they were.

One middle-aged man struggled between being nice and respectable or unconventional and real. In the course of his search he had a dream:

> *There are two boys on a raft floating down a river. One boy is fully clothed, dressed in expensive attire. The other is completely naked. The river starts flowing faster. They realize there are rapids ahead and beyond the rapids a dangerously high waterfall. Their only escape lies in swimming to safety. The naked one dives in and makes the shore. The clothed one doesn't want to ruin his clothes, so he stays with the raft.*

69

The issue was clear: to stay with the male role of hiddenness was to be destroyed; to go with the human response of openness was to make connection.

When an i of a man becoming feels uncomfortable, he allows the uncomfortableness. Consequently he experiences the exhilaration of moving into and through and out from the valley of threat. Seeing and sensing and sharing and exploring and expressing and cooperating and collaborating and cherishing and celebrating flow out and around.

I suspect our human fear of finding who we are comes from our fear of finding what's inside. So we desperately try to keep the lid on how we feel and what we do. Like the older boy we remain shut-up, cautious, calculating, anxious over being anxious. Like the older boy we harden ourselves. Like the older boy we avoid experiencing the consequences of what we ourselves have chosen. Like the older boy we end up miserable, bitter, frustrated, cheated, alienated.

Part of our plight stems from not taking seriously the reality of our creation. We have been made in the image of God. That image is good! At our core, life is orderly and creative, constructive and affirmative, growing and caring. Hurt and anger and violence and lust only mask the deeper longings for relatedness and respect, tenderness and trustworthiness. We are made as a necessary and meaningful part of this world.

If, like the young man, we can experience this inner reality, we grow open in our actions. We take responsibility for what we do. We cultivate our senses. We learn what we do not want. We wake up to what we really want. Then, we find the courage to face what makes us anxious. Self-disclosure leads to self-discovery. And as we discover who we are, we uncover our *human* image.

That fear of finding what's inside was portrayed by Graham Greene in his play, *The Potting Shed*. After years of family deception, there comes the agony of truthful disclosure. There had been a murder in the potting shed, in the greenhouse. The family had covered up that horror for years. One of the members of the family describes a dream that catches up the terror of discovery and the distortion of reality:

> "I've had such a funny dream. I was going down the path to the potting shed, and there was an enormous lion there fast asleep."

A lion, of course, symbolizes violent, destructive inner power.

> "What did you do?" someone asked.
> "I woke it up."
> "Did it eat you up?"
> "No, it only licked my hand."[8]

You see, the end result of becoming who we are is not destruction but life, not misery but mirth, not isolation but comradeship, not fear but trust, not rejection but acceptance, not resentment but reunion. The lion lies down with the lamb. We discover that when we move into life we end up celebrating life.

"Let us eat and make merry; for this my son was dead and is alive again; he was lost and is found!"

A boy grows up to be a man!

FIVE

To Be An i—As A Human

How does a child become a person?

Thus the question of a new i can be asked by human liberation. It implies the backdrop of the old me of how a child becomes childish: babying and baby things, toys and treats, no's and naughtiness, yes's and acceptance, agreeable and conforming. And—

> A person's place is definite and set/A person never gets angry/A person always talks sense/Reasonable people act reasonably/It's a person's duty to do what is expected/A person doesn't make waves/A person does not get hurt and does not hurt others/Persons give themselves to others/A person never makes mistakes/Persons know what's right/A person is perfect. . . .

Person-child in the promised land!

The answer in the human liberation movement of how a child becomes a person would be:

> When one defines one's life and stops being controlled by either inner drives or outer demands. When one learns to be as oneself *and* to be part of the whole—because one has learned

that one's problems are not just one's own.
All over the world, children are growing up. . . .

In the conflict between the old me and a new i, we experience the clash of opposites. Eve's curiosity disturbs Adam's stability. Martha's routine collides with Mary's responsiveness. The younger son's outburst undermines the older boy's order. Part of us feels real identification with Adam and Martha and the elder boy. We can see ourselves in them all too easily. Another part of us feels real sympathy with Eve and Mary and the younger son. We can sense our own longings in them only too clearly.

In truth, each woman and each man dramatize the contrasting and competitive sides of our own total personality. If we think of ourselves primarily as a "male" or a "female," we perpetuate the distortion of language and life, for then we imagine we are what we say we are—the label. We grow preoccupied with the word image of ourselves and the word images of others. And the confusion between word and reality fosters the deepest and most dangerous alienation of all.[1]

To be human, however, clearly means to be split inside. We experience the tension between the routine and the responsive, the structured and the spontaneous, order and outburst, love and will. We know the pressure between keeping things going and keeping life growing. We struggle to balance the means of living and the meaning of life.

Our human split between the old me and a new i can be sensed in the experience of an eight-year-old boy in play therapy. The youngster had a puppet character named "Noodlehand." Noodlehand would politely say "hello" and then promptly bite a person on the nose or chop him up and make him eat bees and spiders.

After a few months, a new puppet character appeared named "Superhand." Superhand was very powerful. He hated evil and evildoers, but because he lived in "Outer Space" he usually was not around when Noodlehand acted up.

One day, after a ferocious battle between the two, the therapist asked the boy, "Whom do you want to win, Noodlehand or Superhand?"

"I don't know! If Noodlehand wins, everything will be terrible—I'll be a mean trouble-maker and nobody will like me. But if Superhand wins, I'll be the best little boy in the whole United States and then everybody will step on me and take advantage of me! I don't know! I don't know!"

The therapist and the boy stood for a long time. Noodlehand was weak from the fight but still alive. Then the therapist said, "Maybe nobody has to win. Maybe Noodlehand can stay around to keep people from stepping on you, and Superhand can move in from Outer Space so he can be around to keep Noodlehand from going too far."

The boy looked at him with a surprised smile. "Maybe," he said.

The next week a new puppet character appeared who began to make peace efforts between Noodlehand and Superhand. His name was "Hand-in-Hand."[2]

Now we have to ask questions: Is such reconciliation between concern for oneself and concern for others merely coincidental, or does it show something of the very nature of humanity itself? Is such reconciliation the result of our own self-conscious efforts, or does it suggest a deeper reality in which we participate but which we do not create? Is such reconciliation a forced togetherness, or does it express the genuinely human?

I suggest that "hand-in-hand" points toward that which the Christian faith has been affirming in Jesus who is called the Christ. In him we discover that "hand-in-hand" discloses "God-in-human" and "human-in-God." In Jesus the Christ we see what God is like and what we are like.

The church came to the conviction that in Jesus Christ we see most clearly that which is present everywhere. We are freed to break away from merely looking at ourselves. We get an outside reference from which to see ourselves more fully. Jesus Christ provides us with the secret that unlocks the mystery of divine presence. The true nature of God is reconciling, healing, suffering care. In Christ we see that reality fully, decisively, without distortion. For the first time in history we no longer have to guess what God is like. We see face to face: initiating love.

But to see God's image in the flesh is to see ourselves as we are made to be. In Jesus the Christ we become conscious of the genuinely human. In him there is neither male nor female, neither majority nor minority, neither in nor out; in him is one whole person, authentic humanity (see Galatians 3:28). That is why the New Testament invites us to grow up every way into the fullness of the measure of the stature of Jesus Christ, to mature humanness (see Ephesians 4:13). As the early church father Irenaeus put it, he became (flesh and blood) as we are in order to make us (genuinely human) as he himself is.[3]

Jesus as human is decidedly together—centered—even as he is definitely in touch—encompassing all. By learning who Christ is we begin to learn who we are. We no longer have to guess about our human image. We see face to face.

But what do we see in him that is new rather than old? What does our discovery of the genuinely human mean? In place of the old me, what is the new i?

AUTHENTIC WITHOUT OVERPOWERING

A first clear impression is that of a powerful person. He presents an intensity of personal presence that commands the center of attention. No matter where he is nor what he is doing, people know he is there.

At the age of twelve he holds seminary professors spellbound with questions and insights. Later on, when he speaks, people listen. He comes across, they say, not as a teacher who always quotes others but as an authority who knows firsthand.

Whether he attends a wedding party or a church service, whether he engages in political discussion or theological controversy, he is always found in the middle. Nobody can miss his presence. He is a powerful person.

At the same time he never seems to overpower. He never rides roughshod over others. In fact, he refuses every expression of authoritarianism. He rejects every effort to set himself up as an unquestioned authority. He refuses to be an uncriticized leader. He denies any suggestion that he is the end in himself. He does not insist upon being recognized.

His friends continually argue over who is going to sit on either side of him at the head table. Jesus reminds them that real greatness is not obsessed with tooting its own horn. Real greatness does not insist upon special privileges. Real greatness is found in building up the inner life of others, not in demanding that others build up one's own inner life.

Instead of an autocratic dictator we find an authentic leader. Instead of an exploitative calculator we sense a real respecter of his own capacities as well as others.

The clearest expression of his power is experienced in his crucifixion. Here he refuses to overpower. Here is affirmation devoid of aggression. Here is the authentic stripped of authoritarianism. Here is no superman, a Clark Kent in a business suit who, when the going gets rough, overwhelms people with his strength.

Rather, behold the new i of the genuinely human.

UNCYNICAL CRITICALNESS

A second clear impression is that of a critical person. He pulls no punches. He softens no blows. He hits hard and he hits straight.

In addressing his home church, he tells them God is more concerned with the outsiders than he is with the insiders. In the days of the great famine God took care of the foreigner, the alien, the nonreligious rather than his own people. Jesus refuses to agree with them that they and their way of life are the most precious of all. Their reaction to his critique is to break up the service. They grab him, drag him through the streets in search of a place to lynch him.

When people clamor to jump on his bandwagon, he tells them: "Not everyone who says to me, 'Lord, Lord,' shall enter the kingdom. In fact, many will come from Asia and Africa and sit down at the banquet table while the sons of America and Europe will be thrown into outer darkness."

A pillar of the church invites him home for dinner. Jesus does not go through the proper ritual before eating. His host is astonished. Jesus says to him: "You church people clean the outside of the cup and the dish, but inside you are full of deception and deceit. You fools! Woe be unto you, for you give a tenth of your income and time to charitable purposes, yet you neglect justice for the oppressed and love for the unlovable and compassion for the disorganized. These you ought to have done, without neglecting your tithe of time and money.

"Woe be unto you," he continues, "for you love the prestige seats in the church; you enjoy making a great spectacle in public; you delight in being addressed as reverend and doctor and pastor. Woe be unto you, hypocrites! For you are like graves which are not seen, and men walk over them without knowing it."

Conservatives complain about Jesus' being too free and easy in the company he keeps. He reminds them: "You criticize John the baptizer for being too rigid. You call him an ascetic and say he is possessed by a devil. Then you jump on me for going to parties and enjoying life. You accuse me of being a glutton and a drunkard. We piped, and you did not dance. We wept, and you did not mourn. Nothing can satisfy you!"

Jesus is painfully critical. I wince each time I read him. There is a grim realism in every observation. Herod is a fox, and he calls him a fox. A rich man wants to follow him, and Jesus tells him he does not have the inner strength. He strikes the final blow when he goes to the great cathedral. He walks in, throws over the literature racks, dumps the collection plates on the floor, and drives out the officials, calling them a bunch of robbers preying on the poor.

Yet in spite of his criticalness I sense no cynicism. It is as though every criticism rises out of a deeper compassion and a deeper concern. Again and again we read, "When he saw . . . he had compassion."

A woman pushes through the crowd simply to touch his coat. When she fearfully owns up to the fact, he says, "Take heart, daughter; your faith has made you whole."

The defenders of decency drag to him another woman whom they caught in the act of adultery. They want to know whether he tolerates such disgraceful behavior. And he gives back to them what they tried to give to her. "Let him who is without sin among you throw the first rock." When everyone shamefully withdraws, Jesus looks at the woman and says: "Is no one left to condemn you? Neither do I. Now go and do not hurt yourself again."

At a formal dinner party a prostitute breaks in and washes his feet with expensive perfume. The host is shocked. What embarrassment! He is outraged. "If you were a prophet," he shouts, "you would have known who she was and the kind of woman she is!"

Jesus answers him: "Simon, I have something to say to you. The greater the debt one person owes to another the greater the gratitude when the debt is wiped out. Those who have been forgiven much are able to love much. Those who love much have been forgiven much."

Instead of an aggressive bully we see a straightforward assertor. Instead of a bludgeoning judge we experience a realistic expresser of the truth of situations.

When Jesus is critical, I sense no personal rancor, no personal vindictiveness, no cynicism. He bears no grudges. When he cuts, he cuts with the same care and concern of a surgeon removing a tumor.

ACCESSIBLE YET AUTONOMOUS

78

A third clear impression of the new i of the genuinely human is the accessibility of Jesus. We constantly find him with others.

He is surrounded by people: young and old, poor and rich, weak and strong, educated and uneducated, women and men. Wherever he goes, they come. He sits down to a meal, and people crowd around. They ask questions; they want insight; they long to be healed. When grown-ups are irritated by children milling around, he reminds them, "Don't stop the youngsters, for of such are true Reality."

Then he turns from the adults to sit down to talk with the children. They climb on his lap. They tell him about the pretty yellow dandelion they picked in the yard. They show him the wiggly worm they pulled out of the ground. And, best of all, they describe for him their new Raggedy Ann tea set.

We find him with people everywhere. He enjoys their presence. He revels in their company. He responds to their needs. He is so accessible.

Yet he is so autonomous. There is a solitariness about him. He can be so withdrawn, so independent, so alone. In the early morning, before the household stirs and the streets bustle, he walks out into the country. No one is around. There in the quietness and solitude he prays. When his friends find him, they urge him to return. People are looking for him. He refuses. "I must be going on to the next town to let them know of the good news also."

At another point the disciples return from preaching and teaching and healing. They are bubbling over with excitement. He interrupts their enthusiasm. He tells them, "Come away by yourselves to a lonely place and rest awhile." We are told that so many people were coming and going that the disciples had no time to eat, let alone to collect their thoughts.

Instead of an anxious weakling, we sense a genuine empathizer who does not confuse his life with others' lives. Instead of being a clinging vine, we see an appreciator of his own and others' being. He can come close without being swallowed up. He can move away without becoming cut off.

Much of the time Jesus is with others, yet much of the time he is with himself. He is so accessible and yet so independent. He relates to others yet reflects himself. He stands with others yet is his own person.

CONSERVER OF THE CREATIVE

A further clear impression of Jesus is his confirming the old by giving birth to the new.

Some have claimed that Jesus attacks tradition to destroy it. Freedom from all restrictions is said to be his call. But I find no such pattern.

Jesus is not a rebellious rebel. He does not throw out values and practices that have developed over a period of time. Every sabbath we find him worshiping in the synagogue. Not one dot of an "i" in the intricate Jewish law is to be cancelled, he insists. When a Pharisee asks what he must do to be whole, Jesus replies, "What is written in your law?" When the surprised man recites the commandments, Jesus concludes, "Do that and you shall live."

At another point he corrects a possible misimpression: "Do not think that I have come to do away with tradition. I have not come to destroy but to fulfill." In terms of the wider demands of government, he indicates that a person is not to give offense but is to pay the required taxes.

At no point do we find Jesus rebelling against his heritage. He is always in the mainstream of community life. He confirms the importance of the structures of society by participating in them.

Yet we find him moving into those structures in ways that break them open. He transforms old me's into new i's. He liberates the life force they seek to express. He is criticized for healing on the sabbath because healing is work and no work is allowed. He explains his action on the basis of the deep principle behind all regulations. Sabbath rest is intended to revitalize life. It is meant for good and not ill. Since the occasion arose to heal, to do so is to fulfill the inner intent of the law and so give glory to God. Rules are made to help us, not to hinder us. Structures are made for people, not people for structures.

What matters, he insists again and again and again, is not outward conformity but inward commitment. Jesus identifies with what matters, with essential goodness within culture. Yet he insists upon openness to unfolding experience. He points toward the freshness of every specific moment. He conserves the heart of the old by discovering the creativity in the new.

Instead of a nice guy who gushes, we find a care-er who works with others. Instead of a paternalistic protector, we experience a creative guide.

80 THE NEW i OF HUMAN

Initially, I asked what do we discover in Jesus the Christ as clues to the new i of the genuinely human? We have found an authentic presence that does not overpower. We have found a critical responsiveness that expresses compassionate concern. We have found an accessibility that does not lose individuality. We have found a conservation of the creative in every situation.

There are other contrasts that strike us as we read the account of his presence: courage with sensitivity, a flexible single-mindedness, a loving lovableness among others.

Each of these genuinely human qualities seems so contradictory. Yet underneath I am conscious of an inner unity, a simplicity, a wholeness of life and purpose. These are not compromised contrasts. These are not watered down qualities that lose the hotness of heat or the coldness of cold in a lukewarm insipidness.

Each is an intense and genuine aspect of his person. Perhaps that is why Jesus says to become like little children: transparent in attitude, spontaneous in action, open and without deception, present without concealment, participating without inhibition.

Adam and Eve, Martha and Mary, elder boy and younger son! Each set is quite clear in its human quality: ordering and bursting out, reliable and responsive, structured and spontaneous—yet all held together in a whole human being.

Since God is whole, we discover we can be whole and are meant to be whole. The puppet character "Hand-in-Hand" is not a forced reconciliation of conflicting desires in an eight-year-old boy in play therapy. "Hand-in-Hand" lights up not only the deepest reality in which we all participate, but also the deepest reality that we ourselves do not create. "Hand-in-Hand" reminds us of God-in-human and human-in-God, even Jesus the Christ.

In him we find the meaning of the genuinely human. In him we see the old me transformed into a new i. In him we know what we truly are.

i Yet Not I

If I am not for myself,
who will be for me?

But if I am only for myself,
what am I?

       Hillel

I am crucified with Christ:
nevertheless I live;

yet not I,
but Christ liveth in me. . . .

    Galatians 2:20, KJV

May God himself, the God of peace,
make you holy in every part,
and keep you sound in spirit, soul, and body. . . .
>   1 Thessalonians 5:23, NEB

The wolf shall live with the sheep,
and the leopard lie down with the kid;
the calf and the young lion shall grow up together,
and a little child shall lead them. . . .
>   Isaiah 11:6-7, NEB

. . . to create out of the two
a single new humanity . . . thereby
making peace. . . .
>   Ephesians 2:15, NEB

SIX
Getting My i Together

I began this study by asking, "Who are you?"

Not only did I want to see our several selves, but even more I wanted us to contact as centered selves.

The reaction of an *objective-me* to the question of identity is no answer, as one person's reaction to my request at the start of a semester to indicate on a 3″ x 5″ card anything about oneself that I ought to know for us to contact through the course in ways that would be mutually beneficial. He wrote:

Who are you?
Write it on a little white card.
Name . . . Sex . . . Race . . .
Place of birth . . . Date of birth . . .
Put it in your job application,
Your school application.
Single . . . Married . . . Widowed . . . Divorced . . .
Put it on your passport,
Your church membership card.
Hobbies . . . Interests . . . Social Security number . . .
Military experience . . . doggy tags . . .
Put it on your voter's registration card . . .
Joys . . . disillusionments . . .
Have you ever been arrested?
Put it on your little white card.
Put it on your driver's license registration.

Have you ever been in a hospital for a nervous disorder?
Prizes . . . awards . . . honors won . . .
Write them all accurately, truthfully, chronologically.
Criminal,
Victim,
Sinner,
Saint.
Please print.
Fill the form in duplicate
And send it in by Tuesday.
Read the instructions carefully.

Who are you?
A universe,
A speck of nothing.
Write it on the little white card.

What comes through is passionate frustration and powerful anger. How can one's full humanness be reduced to pieces of information itemized like a grocery list!

The reaction of the *old-me* to the question of identity is no answer, as Adam-and-Eve and Martha-and-Mary and elder-boy-and-younger-son suggested. The routine order of Adam-and-Martha-and-elder-boy clashed with the spontaneous outburst of Eve-and-Mary-and-younger-son.

Not facts about us nor fragments of us are enough to know for our becoming genuinely human. Some new presence is required. The old me must be transformed by a new i.

In Jesus the Christ we glimpse that new i, that new being, that new world, that new order: the old life is over; a new life has already begun (see 2 Corinthians 5:17). What used to be so separated has now been brought together. The parts complement each other. The several are now single, destroying the dividing wall of hostility, to create one new humanity (see Ephesians 2:13-18). The old me with its divisions and distinctions has now broken down. A new i with its diversity and distinctives has appeared. The many are one. In the genuinely human being one *is* everything and one is *in* every part (see Colossians 3:10-11).

Me-ness + new-ness = i-ness

But how do we move from the "there" of our several selves to the "here" of our single self? How do we transform—change—the "then" of the old me into the "now" of a new i? How, in short, do we get our "i" together as genuine human beings?

If we *are* everything and *in* every part, then we must recontact that which has been cut off, torn apart, and kept separated. We are to experience our i in all of its richness and its vividness, in its concreteness and its complexity. We are to reestablish the foundation of our identity. The truer way of i as subject replaces the former way of me as an object. The strange and the stranger *are* me and "my" other (see Leviticus 19:33-34). Incarnation means new creation!

EXPERIENCING A NEW i AS EVERYTHING

I begin with the conviction that a new i *is* everything. Translated that might mean: "i am the world/the world is i"; "what is is i/i am what is"; "to be is to be all/to be all is to be."

This sounds so mystical, so general, so abstract. So, let's try to become as grounded and concrete as possible. Let's begin with our body, for this is our base, our foundation, our temple (see 1 Corinthians 6:19-20). When we are out of touch with it, we are out of touch with reality.

The Adam-and-Martha-and-elder-boy part of us gets cut off from that awareness of me-ness plus new-ness that equals i-ness. One whole part of us lacks personal participation. The sensory enjoyment of fruit being a delight to the eyes and delicious to the taste or the stimulating excitement of contact with a real person or the sensual participation in rejoicing and festivity are deadened and denied. We become lost because of *our* ignorance and *our* insensitivity. Thus, we need ways of knowing and of sensing the incarnate life God has given us.

Some suggestive exercises in sensory awareness may enable us to contact that basic substance. These require us—

to attend to specific detail,
to act through bodily movement,
to accept responsibility for what we do.

Thus, we become open to experiencing!

Sensory awareness allows us to let go of our stranglehold on life. It enables us to get in touch with reality. We shift our attention from the words to the actual. Too often we think we feel when in fact we fail to feel. We so tighten our hold on life that we lose touch with the life that is ours. Examples of sensory awareness would include: relaxation, breathing, listening, touching, tasting, smelling, moving. Whether engaged in separately or in various combinations, the methods guide us back to our senses.[1]

One of the most basic distinctions is that between bodily tension and bodily relaxation. We could sense that contrast in Adam's conservation and Eve's curiosity, in the elder boy's tightness and the younger son's looseness, in Martha's harriedness and Mary's casualness. We saw that contrast in Jesus' capacity both for criticism and compassion, both for autonomy and accessibility, both in his powerfulness and in his humbleness.

The old me tends to be tense when it ought to be relaxed and relaxed when it ought to be tense. A new i, in contrast, can be tense when tension is called for and relaxed when relaxation is fitting. So we need to learn to discriminate between our bodily states of relaxation and tension. By listening to and learning from our body, we can experience and encourage a new i. We then become a more definite center, realizing that which we already are.

To be at ease increases life and liveliness. When we are relaxed, we expend only the amount of energy necessary to do what has to be done. This lets us do what is done more effectively as well as save energy for other things waiting to be done. When we are comfortable, our entire body works properly: blood flows without hindrance; nerves respond with alertness. In fact, because we flow with experience instead of fighting it, everything becomes more meaningful.

The first step in learning how to relax is to become aware of our tension. Tightness is a message telling us to "let go." That's right, "telling us," for the next step is to become aware of the fact that *we* are causing the tension. Though it may be done below the level of consciousness, tension is still *our own* doing.

The third step is to find out how we create and hold these tensions: For instance, are we rigid in our chest? Do we exert too much pressure in our jaws? Is our stomach tied up in knots? The final step is to let go. We do this best by experiencing the tension instead of avoiding it. We are to move toward the tension, find out what it is saying to us. If we really can listen and learn, then the tightness disappears. We can use our energy as we need it.

What follows is intended to suggest how you can achieve a deep state of relaxation.[2] It will sharpen your awareness of muscular tension and muscular relaxation. This may enable you to be more truly that body that you in fact are.

Read over the instructions and then carry them out. Perhaps, better yet, have someone read them to you as *you do them.* Each

88

step is to be done slowly and fully, making certain you come to attend to and experience *your* body. You are to become incarnate yourself!

Take off your shoes. Loosen any clothing which is binding or which constricts circulation.

Lie back on the floor. Close your eyes. Get comfortable. Uncross your legs. Let your arms and hands go limp.

Become aware that you are thinking and for a few moments observe your thoughts.

Now become aware of bodily sensations. Experience the floor and your relationship to it.

Spend the next few moments listening to the noises in the room.

Become aware of the air that surrounds your body, especially in the exposed areas: your hands, your neck, your face.

Now attend to your breathing. For a few minutes become aware of how you are breathing.

Breathing is a very direct way of relaxing. When breathing is calm, we are quiet. When breathing is agitated, we are agitated. When breathing is paralyzed, we are paralyzed. Natural breathing is a function of the entire body. It is not something that we have to do; rather, it is to be allowed to happen. Minute changes in breathing have a great effect on how we experience the world. When we hold our breath, we avoid emotion and excitement; but the price is anxious living. When we breath naturally, we experience emotion and excitement; the reward is more abundant life.

Make no effort to change your breathing. Just watch it. Let it be what it is. Just let yourself breathe, easily, quietly, naturally.

To achieve a state of deep relaxation I will direct you alternately to contract and relax specific muscles or groups of muscles. In contracting them, do so as fully as you can. Make the muscles tense; make them hurt. In relaxing them, let go all at once. Do not force them. Just let them go. Just let them relax themselves. We will start with the feet and work upward.

89

Curl your toes away from you. Feel the muscles in the arch of your feet tighten. Notice how uncomfortable that feels. Hold it.

Now relax. Notice the difference between the tension and the relaxation.

Now arch your toes upward toward your face. Feel the muscles contract along your shin bones. Make them tight and hard. Hold it.

Now relax. Let your toes and ankles go completely limp. Notice the difference.

Next, flex your thighs. To do this, press your heels down hard against the floor. Press harder. Tighten up the thigh muscles. Really squeeze them hard. Make them ache.

Now relax.

This time tighten the muscles in your buttocks. Raise yourself upward. Squeeze those muscles more. Make them very tight. Keep contracting them.

Now relax. Again, notice the difference between the tension and the relaxation.

Now, without tensing your legs, concentrate on your stomach muscles. Pretend I am going to hit you in the stomach. Make those muscles very tense and taut. Draw them up into a knot. Make your stomach hard. Keep contracting it.

Now relax. Let go, completely. Notice how good it feels to be relaxed.

Now with your body straight, dig in your heels and arch your back. Lift your whole body. Make your lower back quite hollow. Feel the tension all along your spine.

Relax. Settle down on the floor again. Get comfortable. With each exercise try to become aware of the differences between what you feel when you are tense and what you feel when you are relaxed. Just let go. Allow the muscles to hang loose. Nothing is to be supported.

Without increasing the tension elsewhere, form fists with each hand. Squeeze hard. Harder. Really tighten up your hands. Now bend your elbows. Flex your biceps. Hold them rigid. Pull hard. Harder.

Now relax, completely. Let your hands fall where they will. Just let go. Experience the difference.

Now stay completely relaxed; only this time take a very deep breath. Really fill up your lungs. Hold it. Notice how uncomfortable it feels.

Exhale, completely. Let it all out. Notice the calmness that comes with exhalation.

Just breath normally, in and out, regularly, deeply. Notice the difference between the tension and the relaxation.

Now while you maintain this relaxed state, bend your neck back and press your head against the floor. Very hard. Contract the muscles in the back of your neck. Make them hurt. Feel the discomfort.

Relax.

Now bend your head forward. Touch your chest with your chin. Hold it. Notice the discomfort.

Again relax. Again notice the difference between the tension and the relaxation. Attend to both. Be aware of both.

To finish this exercise in bodily sensation, I want you to concentrate on your facial muscles. Remember to keep the rest of your body relaxed. Now clench your jaw. Bite hard. Grit your teeth—harder, so your neck muscles jump. Hold it. Feel the muscles in your cheek contract.

Let go. Relax. Notice the difference.

Next, open your mouth. Real wide. Really stretch it out. Notice the tension in your jaw and neck.

Now relax. Close your mouth. Pay attention to the contrast.
Screw up your eyes. Close them. Squeeze them really hard. Tighter. Feel the discomfort in your eyelids.
Now relax. Keep noticing the difference. Relax your whole face. More. More. Feel the comfort throughout your whole body. Make sure no tension has crept back in.
Now pay attention to your breathing for a moment. See if you can slow it down just a bit. Even it out. Breathe a little more deeply. Breathe a little more slowly. Try to relax your entire body. Relax. Deeper. Deeper. Just relax and enjoy the comfort of relaxation.
Now sit up. Take a few moments to look around the room. You are at-home, at-ease, at-one.

Such experiencing of bodily awareness enables us to know who we are. We get in touch with what *we* want, what *we* need, what *we* intend, what *we* decide, what *we* do. Once we are based in the being of our bodies, then we can become in the doing of every act. We transform the old rigid me into a new responsive i. Everything belongs to us: the world, life and death, the present and the future (see 1 Corinthians 3:21-23).

EXPRESSING A NEW i IN EVERYTHING

Perhaps even more basic than contacting our center is communicating with our complexity—that is, we are so full of life that no single part of us can contain all of us. The several selves of the old me are, in truth, the many-splendored parts of a new i (see Colossians 1:16-17). But to experience that fullness we need to enter into each and every part. We must allow each and every part to become truly part of us.

Under old reality, Adam is in conflict with Eve, the elder boy with the younger son, Martha with Mary. Part against part. Place against place. Person against person.

In new reality, Adam-and-Eve, elder-boy-and-younger-son, Martha-and-Mary are reconciled. Part with part. Place with place. Person with person. One genuinely human reality. Jesus Christ as all in all!

If we are in the parts, then the parts are expressing us. To recover the integrity—that oneness of being—we are to reestablish communication between the parts. Like the demon-possessed man, we are to find in the pieces our peace—my reality (name) is Legion, for I am in many pieces (see Mark 5:9-10, 15). By repossessing what we have split apart and thrown away, we reestablish who we are. By entering into conversation with the separated and segregated, we realize a deeper and more inclusive humanity.

Fritz Perls[3] pioneered in developing techniques to recover those parts of ourselves which we have cut off from our workaday personalities and projected onto other people and things. As one *is* one's projections, one *becomes* oneself. His approach is known as gestalt therapy. "Gestalt" is a German word meaning whole, constellation, configuration, the relationship of the parts to the pattern and the pattern to the parts. Gestalt techniques are ways of integrating competing complexity into a complementary whole.

In the approach every "it" becomes an "i." The past is made present. One's having—passive—fragments of experience turns into one's being—active—the fragments of experience. What presents itself as incomplete and uncomfortable is entered into imaginatively in order to complete it and discover its comfortableness. Thus, those aspects of ourselves that we have overlooked or neglected or rejected are brought back into active relationship with those aspects that we have overstressed or exaggerated or clung to. The isolated parts become parts of a whole.

What I am suggesting is initially difficult as well as confusing. General principles are not enough; something more concrete is needed. As a way to convey the approach, let me use a specific illustration. I turn to part of an exchange between Perls and a woman, Mary Anne, in a seminar on dreams.[4] What he says and has her do in response to her dream shows both the process and the results of the process.

In the dream Mary Anne sees herself standing on a steep cliff overlooking the ocean. Cows with horns start coming out of the water accompanied by their little calves; a man yells at them and they go back. She decides to go swimming. A bedraggled cow-herding dog grabs her hand in its jaw, not biting but just holding firmly.

Perls engages Mary Anne in acting part of the dream as if it were in the present—here and now. He gets her to express her resentment to the man for not letting the cows come out. She answers as the man who knows best about the cows. Soon Perls has her actively *being* the cows and the man and God, who is discovered when she is being hit by the experience.

Mary Anne can really identify the cow and the man and the

onlooker and the little dog as being herself. But the ocean somehow grows insidious, yet it seems to offer protection. When she says she cannot identify with the ocean, Perls picks that up and the following dialogue ensues:

PERLS: You can't identify? Say this to the ocean.

M.A.: I'm sorry, ocean. I just don't dig you. I don't feel that I'm you. I feel that you *engulf* me—I want to get rid of you, this waving ocean, all that you do to me—the salt water that gets in my nose. And yet, this ocean is—kind of loving, and nice, and slippery, and—I don't know if *I* am loving, slippery—Maybe I could be the ocean. I am the ocean. I am loving and slipping over you cows, and there's some seaweed that's around, that you can eat. And some sea otters to give you a little entertainment. And, I *am* the ocean, because the ocean—I am everything being the ocean. I cover—but I know I don't really, because I know there's that land up there, and there's that man with the horn—I guess that the real problem is the man and the ocean.

PERLS: The ocean representing what, and the man representing what?

M.A.: I don't know. The man, I—sort of, think of as my father—a controlling, repellent force that I *want* to go to, and yet I don't want to go to. And the ocean, I think. I . . . it's awfully hard for me to feel this ocean. I don't know what this ocean is—what *you* are, ocean. I don't know what you are. But, partly, you're going to suffocate me, and I think that this ocean is *much* harder for me to deal with than this man. Then I think, well—the ocean is my mother, but then—maybe, this is true, though. Maybe this ocean is—very slippery and—

PERLS: . . . To me, it seems the ocean represents your female part, and the other is the male part. It's the female—the *caring, loving* part—and the other is the fighting, domineering, controlling part of you. So, I think you are right when you say those are the two antagonists. So could you have an encounter with these two parts of you?

M.A.: Well, it's a million times easier. The man part: As the man, I boss people around—keep things back, and I've got my feet on the ground, and . . . It's the woman—this is very hard.

PERLS: I want you to just let the man go into the ocean and see what happens.

M.A.: I, the man, go into the ocean?

PERLS: Yes, you as the man.

M.A.: Well, I—as the man, I won't have anything to do with that ocean. But, if you tell me to go in—

PERLS: Yeah. I'm interested in how this man would control the ocean. He can control cows, apparently.

M.A.: I take off my clothes, and I go into the ocean. And I'd just be a little tiny, itty-bitty speck swimming around in that ocean, with all those cows and all that seaweed. I wouldn't amount to a hill of beans, so I'd have to come right out!

PERLS: What would happen if the ocean came to the man?

M.A.: Then the ocean would lose her identity, because she'd have to come up onto the land, and she wouldn't be the ocean anymore—she'd be a little stream. And, I, as the ocean—I don't want to be a little stream. I want to be an ocean. And I, as the ocean, *resent* that man. He's *different* from me. *He stands up,* and *I* spread out. And I don't like anything different.

PERLS: Say this again.

M.A.: I don't like anything different from me. I want to be it all.

PERLS: So, be it all! Be the ocean, and be the man. This is the essence. Instead of having a conflict—either/or—the male or the female—be both. This has been known for ages, that the conflict between the male and female cycle in a person produces neurosis. Integration produces genius. All geniuses have *both* male *and* female aspects. The really mature person is ambidextrous. [One] not only uses both hands, [one] reacts both emotionally and aggressively toward the world.

So there we see the process of getting one's "i" together. From the emotional intensity of the conflict invested in experiencing the separate parts communicating with each other, there comes a growing awareness of an inclusive self. With the awareness of an inclusive self we find new identity, new reality, new being.

Assertion no longer means taking it out on others
    but the courage to be as oneself;
Agreement no longer means giving in to others
    but the courage to be part of the whole.
Reality in identity;
    integrity in identification.

A centered self and a caring self;
   an expressive self and an adaptive self.
The wolf and the lamb lie down together!

Another woman drew pictures of the process of getting her "i" together as she went through the transformation.[5] The pictures help to make the experience more vivid.

At first (figure 1) she peopled her world with the sour old faces of welfare ladies who had surrounded her in her youth and with whom her mother worked.

As the old self began to break apart and the denied vitality showed itself, her world grew more chaotic (figure 2). A dancing array of grimacing masks in wild, devilish, bizarre, and strange shapes assaulted her.

Gradually, the faces of the girls moved in gorilla-like obscurity on the one side and into open trustingness on the other (figure 3).

With time there came the sullen features of prudish old aunts and twisted devils' faces juxtaposed with sensuous and seductively beautiful women, disguised with a black mask (figure 4). The battle between the excessively responsible establishment and the exceedingly neglected expressiveness continued to be waged inside.

Then, there came a time

95

when, like Joan, she molded a female figure. At first it was in the form of a rigid crucifix. She was herself, but fixed and set—paralyzed between pressure from the past and the pull of the future. Eventually, the figure transformed itself— seemingly spontaneously in her hands—into a graceful dancing girl (figure 5). The woman came to the realization, as she said, that God pervades everything, even a whore dancer.

What you see in these pictures is what I have been trying to convey.

In the rigid old me, life is lost because life is partial. All our energy is used to keep life tense.

In a new i, life is found because life is whole. Energy is available for every expression:

> Adam's control *and* Eve's curiosity;
> Martha's responsible routine *and* Mary's responsive spontaneity;
> The elder boy's order *and* the younger son's outburst.

Each is necessary; neither is sufficient. Separated, they make for death. Together, they make for life. That is what blacks mean by "soul"—participation and freedom, well-being and warmth.

The genuine human being appears among us that we, also, might have life and have it "in all its fullness" (John 10:10, NEB). In getting our i together, we get everything and everyone together!

In each of us
the Spirit is manifested
in one particular way,
for some useful purpose.
1 Corinthians 12:7, NEB

Whoever seeks to save his life
will lose it;
and whoever loses it,
will save it and live.
Luke 17:33, NEB

SEVEN
Giving My i Away

The first decisive issue of who I am is getting my i together. The second decisive issue of who I am is giving my i away.

Though everything is truly ours, we truly are not our own (1 Corinthians 3:21-23). We are not meant to end in ourselves nor to stop with ourselves. The more we are the self of a new i the less there is the self of the old me in us. We are ourselves most fully when we transcend ourselves.

In A.D. 200, the martyr Felicitas reminded the fellowship of the faithful of the nature of divine order. She declared: "Another for me and I for him." Less than a century later St. Antony, the first of the Christian hermits, took up his dwelling between the Nile River and the Red Sea. There, alone, ascetic, and emaciated, he gave the church the same formula: "Your life and your death are with your neighbour."[1]

The mistake of Adam and Martha and the elder boy was not in serving others but in denying themselves. Not having an i of their own, they had little i to give away. Not loving themselves rightly, they could not love others genuinely (see Mark 12:28-34). Thus, service by them became a mask-hiding service *of* and *for* them— "tell her to help me"; "you never gave me!" Drawing upon the language of William James, we could say that their "I" wanted harmony with others but their "me" did all it could to prevent it.[2]

The discovery of Eve and Mary and the younger son was not an independent "I" but an interdependent "we." Thus their spontaneity and outburst turned into a way of getting back to others. The apparently big I against and apart from others ended up as a fitting i with and for others.

One man, in his late thirties, put the experience this way:

> For almost a dozen years I thought awareness was spelled ME and was characterized by a Gimme-Gimme-Get-Get-Gimme attitude.
>
> Then for several more years after that I thought awareness was spelled COMMITMENT and was characterized by an aggressive, cut-down, destroy, and rebuild in-the-name-of-Jesus attitude.
>
> But of late I have learned that awareness is spelled LOVE.

To be an i is to be neither the whole show nor an abandoned show. To be an i is to be more than the me. To be an i is to be one through whom life lives. To be an i is to give the me away that every i may be.

> I am crucified with Christ:
>> nevertheless i live;
>>> yet not I,
>>> but Christ liveth in me. . . .
>>>> (Galatians 2:20, KJV)

Here is the seeming paradox of the genuinely human: i, yet not I, but true i. The "i" in the "me."

If the first sign of the genuinely human is a distinct individual identity with integrity, the last sign of the genuinely human is a letting go of that i in identification with and for all humanity. The ultimate mark of the mature human being is this: serving rather than being served, giving rather than getting, ministering rather than being ministered unto, the love of Christ—agape—understanding care for others' needs and well-being apart from one's own needs and well-being.

98

Despite the disciples' protest, Jesus stooped and washed the dust of the road from their feet (John 13:3-17). That act was not womanly nor did it deny the manly. There was nothing of an inferior serving a superior. There was nothing of a superior patronizing an inferior. "I shall not call you servants any more, because a servant does not know his master's business; I call you friends, because I have made known to you everything I have learnt from my Father. . . . What I command you is to love one another" (John 15:15-17, JB). That act demonstrated the genuinely human.

By his own crucifixion Jesus as the Christ—the genuinely human—showed that the most fully human/divine act—the most authentically real and right response—is this: that one give oneself in love to others and for others in ways that matter. The West African crucifixion, shown here, reflects a very local style.[3]

99

La Crucifixion

Groupe en cuivre réalisé en Nigéria. (Afrique Occidentale).

However, it also resembles all the Christs whom Christianity knew for long centuries. Here is a mystical Christ, standing on his cross, with eyes wide open—seeing and understanding—triumphing over suffering and death.

Let's examine that giving an i away in more detail. Here we find the interplay of responsibility, vulnerability, and risk. The self-centered me is transformed into an i-centered self—an i that is not the I of the old me but an i of Christ living within.

RESPONSIBILITY

The most obvious demand which society makes on us is that we be part of the whole. We hear that from family, from friends, from neighbors, from community, from nation. Belong. Participate. Contribute.

At the most superficial level, that means we are not to "rock the boat." We can be different *if* we are neither difficult nor deviant in any way that upsets others. "If you don't like us, leave us. Shape up or get out."

At the deeper level, that demand to be part of the whole means our life is intimately intertwined with the life of all. I in you; you in me. One in the many; the many in everyone. Without you I cannot be; without me you cannot be. We are here together—all together or we are not here at all.

Thus Adam-and-Martha-and-elder boy point toward the necessity of our being responsible for human existence, even though their actions tend to deny that. We are accountable for what happens in our world. The first question of the old me is: What can I demand of life? The basic question of a new i is: What does life demand of me?

Perhaps the greatest tragedy of those who are denied being an i— marginal minorities of whatever kind: young/old, female/male, black/brown/red/yellow/white—is the absence of any expectation and demand that they be a necessary part of life. The need to be needed—whether that need is conceiving and/or nurturing bearers of the future or contributing to the world's requirements for productivity or sharing and supporting another person's experience—that is the deepest demand of identity. We are here to respond responsibly!

The ordering of life, however, is not the set and static order of the overly conforming individual. Rather, it is the flowing and dynamic order of the responsibly creative grown-up. There is always something disorderly in such responsible order, for life is allowed, yes, even encouraged, to break out of every established routine. Order is meant for people, not people for order (see Mark 2:23-3:6). Thus, the acceptance of outburst and the presence of flexibility.

We participate in the ongoing and the everyday, because the life channeled there is *the* life to be ordered. We are not made to take part—forced by parents or by peers. We choose to dig in. We want to belong to the process. We find where the traction is. We invest our life in what we believe in beyond ourselves and our own. No one takes life from the genuinely human, but the genuinely human gives it up of oneself (Mark 10:45; John 10:18).

Such involvement is a far cry from the reluctant and resentful involvement of an elder boy or a Martha. They hung in because they were afraid to take off. They helped out in hopes of being set up. The genuinely human, in contrast, hangs in because one prefers to be here rather than there. The genuinely human helps out in hope that all might be set free sooner rather than later. Such involvement is throwing oneself into the center of things for the sake of the involvement itself. To be here-now is its own reward.

The strangest paradox of all is that when my old me is absolutely free, then I am actually nobody. When my new i is absolutely called upon, then i am definitely somebody. Unless I am responsible for creating order and contributing to the ongoing, I do not exist. Only when I am continually creating order and contributing to the ongoing, do i exist. In hanging on to my me for the sake of myself, I lose my i. In letting go of my I for the sake of others, I find an i. Self-consciousness and self-concern are transcended in awareness of the world and concern for others.

We are created to invest our lives in the lives of others in ways that matter. That may be as simple as a smile or as complicated as a peace treaty. We may prepare another a meal in time of sickness or stay with another's tears in time of grief or share another's anger in an unjust situation or. . . . The ways to give ourselves to others are endless.

The demand to be for others is ultimate.
No life without life together.

VULNERABILITY

For Christians, the crucifixion of Christ is a central symbol of our life in faith. It implies dying to the old realities and discovering a new reality. While it is tied closely with physical death in the outer realm, the experience is intended to deal with the death of the old me in the inner realm. We are confronted with the cross not as a way to death but as a means of life, not for the sake of ending all but for the purpose of finding all.

Paul set forth the issue:

> If we have, as it were, shared his death, we shall also share in his resurrection! Let us never forget that our old selves died with him on the cross that the tyranny of sin over us might be broken—for a dead [person] can safely be said to be free from the power of sin. And if we were dead [people] with Christ we can believe that we shall also be [people] alive with him . . . look upon yourselves as dead to the appeal and power of sin but alive to God through Jesus Christ our Lord.
>
> Romans 6:5-11, Phillips

The unbalancing of the old me comes directly from one of two mistakes. Either we need to be front and center, in short, the whole show and the last word; or we need to be out in back and away from it all, in short, no part of and no say in anything. We are afraid we won't be recognized; we are afraid we will be recognized.

Yet in the power of a new ı we no longer have to be front and center. In the power of a new i we no longer have to be out in back and away from it all. We are free to be here-now. We are free to be vulnerable. We, thereby, regain our balance and contribute to the rebalancing of *our* world.

Crucifixion means

giving up our having to be—
letting go our having to become—
forgetting our having to be ourselves—
foregoing our having to belong—
here and now.

In emptying oneself, one becomes open. "Indeed," points out Erich Fromm, "if one cannot make oneself empty, how can one respond to the world? How can one see, hear, feel, love, if one is filled with one's ego, if one is driven by greed?"[4]

There is no longer the me to protect. There is no longer the self to preserve. There is no longer anything (see Philippians 2:4-8).

The real has become Real. The true has become True. The right has become Right. The trustworthy has become Trustworthy.

All is together.
All is whole.
All is one.

RISK

To be responsible and at the same time to be vulnerable leads to one consequence. To live a new i in Christ is to risk the old me in every place every moment. The spontaneous and the surprising are marks of the Spirit (see Luke 9:57-62; 2 Peter 3:10-13; 1 John 3:2). Only with regular spontaneity can the outburst of really true and trustworthy order be disclosed to us. The life i live is the life of risking all for the sake of all.

The regular and the routine of Martha and the elder boy are right but not real. The spontaneity and the outburst of Mary and the younger son are real but not right. Likewise, the conforming side of us—Adam—has within it that which is trustworthy yet not true. The rebellious side of us—Eve—has within it that which is true yet not trustworthy.

Only within the genuinely human do we see what is real joined with what is right. Only within the genuinely human do we find what is true embodied in what is trustworthy. Only within the genuinely human is being part of the whole integrated with being as oneself. Paul warned:

> If I start building up again a system which I have pulled down, then it is that I show myself as a transgressor of the law. For through the law I died to law—to live for God. I have been crucified with Christ: the life I now live is not my life, but the life which Christ lives in me; and my present bodily life is lived by faith . . . if righteousness comes by law, then Christ died for nothing.
>
> Galatians 2:18-21, NEB

What can be more radical and more risky than that!

We are to give our i away by throwing ourselves into life without reservation. Caution goes. Calculation disappears. We are to hang on to no-thing: no particular order, no particular regulation, no particular person, no particular conviction.

The caring comes. The fitting appears. We are to be in touch with the whole: in every particular order, in every particular regulation, in every particular person, in every particular conviction.

Love requires that will be true; will demands that love be trustworthy.

Love insures that will is real; will makes certain that love is right.

Love actualizes will; will realizes love.

Undergoing a change in his career at fifty-three years of age, Steve provides a glimpse of a new i transforming the old me.

He had been "successful": good job; good marriage; good family; good churchman; good citizen. Yet something was lacking. But what?

Steve had worked to "fit in." Then he realized that he had avoided "uproars, difficulties, estrangement from others, defiance, confrontation and rebellion." Perhaps, he speculated, that was why no one disliked him yet maybe the reason why some people did not respect him.

He had missed "a lot of hassle and undoubtedly a lot of personal discomfort." But he suspected that he had "also missed a lot of possiblities: possibilities to exert changes in situations that needed changing; or possibilities of expanding someone else's awareness of the real nature of a problem; or perhaps, even more important, expanding my own awareness of the breadth and depth of a problem by avoiding getting into the real gut issues and feelings which might erupt from such a confrontation. And so," he concluded, "I'm afraid my obituary is much more likely to read 'nice guy' than 'asserter,' 'pleasant' but not 'performer.' And rightly so."

In stifling his own contribution, he had stifled everyone's contribution. He finally had to ask himself, "What are the missed possibilities, the unactualized potentials, the diluted strengths, the might-have-beens?" He acknowledged that "they are un-questionably numerous, undoubtedly important, and completely unalterable."

Then it was that Steve saw the relevance of the painful process of wrestling with the question of "who am I?" "The only thing that is alterable," he discovered, "from here on is me. Sad though some of my awareness is, self-pity and self-elimination are either a waste of time or a waste of life and both border on being a criminal use of human potential."

With that realization he could more easily experience the grace of the gift of a new i. He could push the past into the past. He could, as Tillich put it, remember to forget.[5] He could begin moving into his own potential.

Steve tried risking on a couple of occasions and was delighted with the results. During a difficult budget-cutting community chest board meeting, he told a man that what the man had said about the agency Steve represented made him very angry. The man blinked; asked why; and the next moment everyone launched into a wide-open discussion of what the real feelings were behind some of the actions that had been taken and explained with a saccharine kind of logic.

The experience gave Steve the courage to risk a spontaneous statement from the floor of a church convention a week later. To his surprise he found support for the cause coming out of the woodwork. "Who knows," he declared, "I can do it some more!"

Steve saw the calculating fearfulness of the old me as one of the chief reasons he had put off his career change. He had not wanted "to risk the uncertainty—just get along—be a pleasant guy—do a good job—but don't raise the big question or you may get the axe—etc." However, he did make the move, did start down *his* road, and "old spilt milk is just about as sour as sour grapes, and neither one is worth anything."

"So," Steve shares, "where do I go from here? Onward certainly, inward acceptingly, outward hopefully, and upward possibly! Perhaps not too bad a choice—four directions but none of them with any absolute limits. The possibilities for expansion stretch toward infinity, perhaps the infinite goal of total self-realization. I'm afraid I'm just a little short of time to reach that goal, but it certainly offers an exciting direction!"

There is no reality in isolated individual identity. To get one's i together finally means to give one's i away in identification with all. The fulfillment of meaning always and ever demands more than the fulfillment of me.

As the great fourteenth-century German mystic Meister Eckhart saw: "In bursting forth I discover that God and I are One. Now I am what I was [meant to be]. . . ." [6]

We are human by virtue of our ability to be inspired to serve.

I do not reckon
myself
to have got hold of it yet.
All I can say is this:
    forgetting what is behind me,
    and reaching out for that which lies ahead,
    I press towards the goal . . . .
                Philippians 3:13-14, NEB

EIGHT

Affirming the Unexpected

In the genuinely human being we have seen wholeness. Such a person beautifully balances closeness and distance, dominance and obedience. Firmness complements sensitivity, assertion caring, directness helpfulness. Outburst discloses order, and regularity reveals spontaneity. Will does not destroy love nor is love lost in will. All holds together (see Colossians 1:17).

If we were to stop there, however, I would be misleading you. I would be setting before you—and myself—an impossible ideal and a crippling illusion: *the* new i. There would be no questions, no uncertainty, no surprise. What it means to be genuinely human would be answered—definitely, decisively, completely. Life would be simple and set forever and ever.

That is what we seek. That is what we want. That is what we expect.

A woman tells me of her conflict with a fellow worker. She looks to the other for support and is hurt (angered) by the other's insensitivity. With some encouragement from me she tells the other how she feels and more important what she is wanting. The air is cleared a little. She begins to experience more strength as a person.

Then she confesses wistfully, "It isn't perfect. I just wish I could get to the point where I no longer become upset; where I would not let little things bother me; where I would no longer be anxious; where everything would be all right."

The beautiful balance of *the* genuinely human being never quite corresponds with the tentative balance of *a* genuinely human me. For we discover in ourselves both the old me *and* a new i, both patterns that we recognize *and* surprises that we do not expect. Because it never fits any specific situation, the ideal is forever unattainable. What we face in every here and now is a unique integration of outburst and order, a particular combination of spontaneity and regularity.

There is no set and single way of being a genuine i.

What I regard as spontaneous outburst you may take to be chaos. What I see as orderly regularity you may view as rigidity. What I take as genuinely human you may find phony and unreal.

What, for example, do you see in the following?[1] Three boxes? Three union jacks? Three confederate flags?

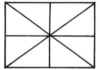 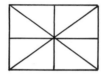

Three geometric designs? Twenty-four triangles? Three pyramids? Your responses suggest a variety of meanings. Suppose I were to say that the above contains every three-letter word in the English language? You may be skeptical, but as you trace a letter in each box, making certain lines stand out and other lines recede, you can begin to sense the possibilities. "Cat," for instance, could look like this:

  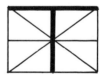

You can figure the rest from there.

Now the question comes: which way of seeing is right? Boxes? Flags? Geometric designs? Triangles? Pyramids? Three-letter words? Which three-letter word? Which way of seeing is correct?

Of course, all of them are "right." Which is correct depends upon the way we arrange the parts into a pattern. What is "there" depends upon what we see as the focus and what we take as the background. The combination of details that makes up the design depends upon what is wanted, even more, upon what is needed in *the specific* situation.

Consider more closely, if you will, the way we put our world together in terms of the ways we see ourselves. Recall how Ruby (in chapter 1) saw herself in a disturbed way and saw her classmate in a healthy way. The whole is always more than the sum of the parts— that is, the character or quality of what we see is always the consequence of the relationship of the parts to the whole. Technically, this is called the figure/ground relationship or the gestalt, a term introduced in chapter 6.

The figure has shape and form. The ground is relatively shapeless and formless. The figure provides the focus of interest and attention. It is out in front and central. The ground provides the setting or context in which something appears. It is vague, unfocused, and on the periphery of awareness. Yet the ground determines the "feel" or "meaning" or "sense" or context of what we see.

In terms of the way we see ourselves—the old me or a new i—look at this picture.[2] What do you see? You may be the one out of five who sees an old woman facing to the left and looking forward with

109

her chin tucked down into a fur piece. On the other hand, you may be among the vast majority who see a young woman in a three-quarters view to the left with a flowing headpiece.

Again, if someone asks which is the right woman, we would have to say: both, depending upon the way one looks at the picture. However, whether one sees the young woman or the old woman, every part belongs either as part of the figure or as part of the ground.

A new and genuine i is made up of all the elements present in the old me. Similarly, the old me is made up of all the elements present in a new i. Both ways of being ourselves are always possible and ever present. Outburst and order, spontaneity and regularity—these are the elements and their relationship to each other determines the way we see and experience ourselves. "It is I who with my reason serve the Law of God, and no less I who serve in my unspiritual self the law of sin" (Romans 7:25, JB).

The presence of outburst and spontaneity, especially, confronts us with decisions about what we do with the unknown and unpredictable elements in our lives, for they represent the powerful elemental forces surging within us—sex and love, anger and rage, power and drive.

Rollo May reports a study of three hundred patients before and after they underwent lobotomies, which are brain operations to eliminate such disruption and stress as rage and terror and lust and violence.[3] Before the operation one of the patients, a doctor suffering with schizophrenia, complained about a recurring nightmare. He was constantly surrounded by wild animals in an arena. After the operation the lions no longer roared, no longer frightened him; they only walked silently away from him. May comments, "When I read this, I was aware of a vague discomfort which I soon realized was the feeling that walking silently away was a potentiality precious to this man's life, and he was the poorer thereby."

Without roaring lions, a person's will is lost. Without roaring lions, a person's love is gone. Precious potentiality disappears. The unexpected, the surprises and the surprising, the vitality of the ever-new-and-fresh and yet-to-be-formed are missing, and life is impoverished.

In the genuinely human, somehow the breaking out of the younger son-and-Mary-and-Eve and the staying with of the elder

110

boy-and-Martha-and-Adam must both be present. To eliminate either aspect destroys the truly and fully human.

But how do lions and life go together? What can it mean to get my i together and to give my i away simultaneously?

Consider the experience of the children of Israel in the wilderness of Sinai.[4] They were in transition between the boxed-in rigidity and lifelessness of being no-body and the breaking-out possibility and liveliness of being some-body.

In the struggle between the old me and a new i they grew discouraged and desperate. Eventually, the strain became intolerable. They cursed God by complaining to Moses: "Why did you bring us out of Egypt to die in this wilderness? For there is neither bread nor water here." In response to their bitter wailing, "God sent fiery serpents among the people; their bite brought death to many in Israel" (Numbers 21:4-9, JB).

Egypt might well stand for every form of enslavement. Whether we are trapped by our dependency, blinded by our racism and sexism, limited by our culture, locked into only one way of seeing life, we are caught in that which curtails and cripples and corrupts our maturing. Unexpectedly, sometimes we find ourselves breaking out of those fixed patterns. But in breaking out, freedom feels more frightening than fascinating. We want to go home again. We want to return to the families. We long to get back to the womblike. We are overwhelmed with anxiety and conflict.

In other words, the account of the children of Israel bitten by serpents is not simply a story of a motley band of refugees from the past. It is even more a portrayal of everyone's struggle to be free, to find wholeness, to become a new and genuine i. The fiery serpents symbolize those powerful forces of life[5]—spontaneity and regularity, outburst and order—that we experience threatening to destroy us.

Clearly, the serpents dramatize the destructive forces in the outer world: racism, war, riots, violence, sexism, age-ism, backlash. They equally dramatize the disruptive forces of the inner world: fear, hate, suspicion, anger, passion, lust, hurt, longing. The fiery serpents meet us in our pilgrimage from slavery to freedom. They confront us in our growth from immaturity to maturity. Isaiah (30:6, JB) described the experience of that wilderness stretch: "the land of distress and of anguish, of lioness and roaring lion, of viper and flying serpent. . . ."

111

From Genesis and the serpent tempting Eve in the Garden to Jonah in the belly of the whale, to Job encountering the great monsters of the deep, to Daniel in the lion's den, to Jesus with the wild beasts in the wilderness, to the great serpent dragon of the book of Revelation, we find this symbolic portrayal of the powerful forces that threaten us from within and without.

Like the people of Israel, we, too, beseech our Moses, the person we look up to, to "intercede for us with Yahweh to save us from these serpents." Get us out of the situations that are uncertain and uncomfortable and upsetting. We want what is certain and comfortable and set.

Our Moses, the person upon whom we depend, opens up the situation on our behalf. And the answer from the source and ground of life is this:

> "Make a fiery serpent and put it on a standard. If anyone is bitten and looks at it, he shall live."
>
> Numbers 21:8, JB

And our Moses makes a serpent of bronze, a symbol of faith, and puts it on a pole. And it comes to pass that when a serpent bites a person and the person beholds the serpent of faith, that person lives.

Our problem with the old me is that in being bitten by the powers of life we die. Our possibility in a new i is that in beholding the powers of life we live. Now this is a strange answer to the issue of identity. What are we to make of it? How are we to take it?

SEE AND ACCEPT

Notice immediately that we are not to avoid the disruptive and unknown. Outburst and spontaneity are always front and center. Anger and rage and love and lust are contact emotions.[6] By means of them we get in touch with life. To look at these powerful passions—really to see the image of destruction in whatever form it appears—averts death and awakens possibility. We come alive.

That, of course, goes against everyday expectations, for we prefer not to look at the unpleasant. We turn away from the sordid, the shameful, the suffering, the sinful. In the face of the frightening we are told, "Don't think about it. Put it out of your mind. Think about something else."

So we cloak the painful in the innocuous or pleasant:

Thus to bomb more hell out of a tiny Asian country in one year than was bombed out of Europe in the whole Second World War becomes "escalation." Threatening to burn and blast to death several million civilians in an enemy country is called "deterence." Turning a city into radioactive rubble is called "taking out" a city. . . . A comparison of the slaughter on both sides in a war is called a "kill ratio." Totaling up the corpses is called a "body count." Running the blacks out of town is called "urban renewal." . . . Outflanking the discontent of employees is called "personnel management." Wherever possible, hideous realities are referred to by cryptic initials and formulalike phrases: ICBM, CBR, mega-deaths, or "operation" this, "operation" that . . . linguistic camouflage to obscure realities.[7]

Funeral customs are designed to cloak the face of death under a mask of life. Deep antagonism between a husband and a wife is veneered with politeness and cordiality. Knowledge of a terminal disease is so diluted that one psychiatrist boasted that he had managed to keep a patient in therapy to the point of death without her ever knowing she was going to die.

We drug the cancerous growth of self or society with a headache pill, grass, or a trip. What is avoided, then, is placed outside of us, and reality then becomes *the enemy*. Not apprehending what's there, we grow increasingly apprehensive over what it means.

A seventeen-year-old freshman girl went into a schizophrenic breakdown. She started throwing things out of the window of her dormitory. She attacked a classmate, broke a mirror, slashed her wrists. She claimed that she was being attacked by "Communists from Mars." So the family, completely baffled by the experience, took her to a therapist.

"We simply can't understand it," her distressed mother told him. "She's never done anything like this before. There's never been any problem of any kind in the family. My husband and I are happily married. Our daughters have always been well and happy."

When the therapist suggested the whole family get together to talk about what was happening, the mother grew upset. She felt the eight-year-old, especially, would be terribly affected; yet the therapist insisted.

When they had assembled—father, mother, Judy, and her sister—the mother reiterated what she had said. "As I told you, we just don't have any problems." "Except," the therapist noted, "for Judy, who's sitting here worrying about Communists from Mars." "But I explained that she's never acted like that," retorted the mother.

At that point the eight-year-old interrupted. "She was too like this before, mother. Remember last Christmas, when daddy didn't come home from his business trip, and you drank too much again and got sick. . . ."

"Within a short time it became obvious that Mrs. Jones was an alcoholic. Later, it also became obvious that Mr. Jones's 'business trips' were actually visits" to another woman in a neighboring city. "The idyllic picture of the Jones family had abruptly shattered."[8]

That is the temptation: everything is nice when everything is nasty; everything is pleasant when everything is painful; everything is settled when everything is upset; everything is working out when nothing is working out. When bitten by the fiery serpents, we prefer not to look.

Yet not to look is to die. To look is to live.

That is the truth Judy illustrates. When underlying family problems came out in the open, she grew quiet and relaxed. Her suicidal threats stopped. Her warnings against Martian Communists ceased. She took part in the conversation, logically and sanely.

A new i demands that we face what we fear. When bitten, we are to look at what bites us. The perils of life—the danger to orderly and routine existence—are compensations for our imbalance. They are attempts to restore our proper balance. What has been lost demands to be found.

LIFT UP AND AFFIRM

God's answer to Moses, however, contains a deeper note than merely looking at the forces of disruption. We came upon a clue to this deeper meaning of identifying with what devours us in a very unusual passage in the Gospel of John (3:14-15, NEB):

> This Son of Man must be lifted up as the serpent was lifted up by Moses in the wilderness, so that everyone who has faith in him may in him possess eternal life.

Bizarre but nevertheless there: the fiery serpents in the wilderness are transformed into the Son of Man on the cross.

We are to take the forces of disruption and affirm them.

A medieval painting pictures the Scripture.[9] Here you see the cross with a great serpent wrapped around the cross in place of Jesus. Moses stands below in the midst of a gathering of church

dignitaries. Two Latin inscriptions refer to the passage in Numbers and the one in John. Thus, the artist brought together the bronze serpent and the crucified Christ in a single symbol. The destructive is now looked at *and* lifted up. That which in the beginning produced death now is seen as that which brings life and wholeness to light.

How can that be? How is it that the forces of disorder can be both agents of death *and* heralds of life? Why must the fiery serpents and the faithful son—the roaring lion and the triumphant lamb—be embraced and affirmed?

Another medieval painting helps us to understand.[10] A hunter is shooting an arrow at the great beast. Instead of the arrow hitting and killing the beast, it turns back and will kill the hunter. The attempt to destroy the beast destroys the person, for the beast represents the vital forces and creative energies of the created world. To deny them is to deny life. To destroy them is to destroy oneself.

The forces of life rise up from the very ground and source of our being. They are the biological base of life.[11] When we deny or avoid their existence, they have the power to take over the whole of our self or society as though by an outside alien force. To deprive ourselves of these natural energies is to deprive ourselves of the very energy of life itself. But when affirmed, the energy is available as the power and purpose of our becoming more genuinely human.

With the vision of the serpent lifted up as the Son of Man we find the courage to struggle for full humanness. The threatening depth pushes us toward the divine height. The more we come to terms with what we fear, the more we find ourselves living by faith.

CONTINUAL RISK

But we must labor under no illusion. The vision of the serpent affirmed is no easy vision. To let life loose in our lives does not guarantee an easy life.

In the book of Revelation, chapter 20, we read of an angel coming down out of heaven, entering the very depths of the deep, and binding the beast for a thousand years of peace. At the end of that aeon, the beast breaks the bonds, again strewing the earth with disruption and destruction. The great serpent is never finally eliminated. As we are told after Jesus' struggle in the wilderness, the disruption left him until another fruitful time (see Luke 4:13).

That imagery suggests the presence of surplus vitality and energy. No life can be content with the life as it is. No order can ever order all there is to order. No routine can ever regularize all there is to regulate. Outburst and spontaneity, the surprising and the unknown, are ever and always present and active. Rebellion against the unjust and the dehumanizing and not indifference or adjustment are evidence of health and hope and faith.[12] The structures we create never can contain the spirit that we are. In our search for wholeness life breaks beyond every form.

We are meant to become richer, fuller, more than we have been or now are. We are not yet "established." We are to "become what we will be!"[13]

What is a fitting response in a five-year-old turns into an inappropriate reaction in a ten-year-old. What speaks meaningfully at one time loses its power to speak at another. The powerful word eventually ends as only a pious platitude or conventional cliche. Inevitably, there come moments when spirit breaks beyond old forms that new life might be expressed.

The kind of workable relationship my wife and I evolved before we had children proved inadequate when those little buzzing, booming, bundles of energy appeared. The kind of workable relationship we then evolved as a family is now giving way as our children grow up and go away. Our channeling of life is always partial, always preliminary, always on the way to what follows after.

The new moment requires new means. The renewing spirit demands new structures. This is a hard word.[14] It means we must constantly be open to disruption from the surprising. Every order eventually grows unstable after it has reached its optimum complexity.[15] Then it dies by coming apart in order that the overlooked and underused elements can create a more fitting order (see Jeremiah 1:9-10). We are to strive after wholeness—"Be ye therefore perfect" (Matthew 5:48, KJV)—but we always find and ever suffer the unsuspected (see Romans 7:21).

The way to being ourselves fully and genuinely predictably passes through the wilderness and the depths. Jonah lay three days in the belly of the whale, which means being caught in the consuming powers of the unconscious. Jesus spent forty days wrestling with the beasts, which again implies struggling with the disruptive outbursts of life forces. As Kierkegaard put it, we must pierce through every negativity if we are to find life, if we are to become that self which we truly are.[16]

The way is never easy. The struggle is never ended. In looking back at her own struggles with anxiety, one woman declared, "When I got through with therapy, I thought I would be all through with trouble. I would be a new person. I would have a new self. But I find that I am still the same old me with the same old problems. Only there is a difference. Before the problems were always on top of me, and now, more often than not, I am on top of them."

That is what we may expect. The old me with its fiery forces and a new i with its person of faith are always present potentially. But, more often than not, we see *and* are a new i. By affirming the unexpected, by celebrating what is our own, a new i appears in place of the old me. The more truly human comes only in and through living the genuinely human.

ALL IS YES, SO YES TO ALL

A next to last word is an including and inclusive word about who one is.

That which we experience as negative represents blocks in our becoming truly whole.[17] These blocks are signals warning us of the need for change. When we can affirm the negative, then the frightening presence of the serpent turns into the comforting presence of the Savior.

While many parts of our experience may be burdensome, all are usable. "We know," Paul pointed out, "that to those who love God, who are called according to his plan, everything that happens fits into a pattern for good" or as the Latin Vulgate translation has it "everything conspires for good . . ."(Romans 8:28, Phillips).

That does not mean everything that happens is good in and of itself. Much that befalls us is not. Rather, faith affirms that no matter what the character of an experience is, it has within the potential to be used for our human becoming. Within every situation—given the gestalt of a new i—we can find some redeeming possibilities. The question we are to address to the surprising and the disruptive is: how can this be used?

God saw *all* that he had made as "very good" and "holy" (see Genesis 1:31; 2:3). Therefore, no part can be excluded or neglected. To be whole, my i must include all.

No individual part of me can be taken as the whole of my i (1 Corinthians 12:14-26). Every individual part of me is necessary for a genuinely new i. Adam-Eve-serpent-God: all parts become part of the whole when we realize a full human relationship with them.

In fact, in the providence of God there is a reversal of the ways we order our world. Not only are those aspects which have been despised and rejected made the key of the real and the right (see 1 Peter 2:7) but also what is nothing at all shows up what appears to be everything and so overthrows "the existing order" (see 1 Corinthians 1:27-28, JB & NEB).

There are two major ways of organizing who we are: that of the old me and that of a new i. The old me turns out to be an increasingly narrow and excluding self. One becomes more and more one way with one pattern, and so one grows less and less able to be part of the whole. A new i grows into an increasingly broad and including self. By becoming part of the whole, one gains more of a world in which to be at-home.

In responding to the issue of "who am I" and the expectation of growing up into full humanity, we discover that because all is YES we can and we must say YES to ALL (see 2 Corinthians 1:19-20)!

Notes

CHAPTER ONE

[1] Soren Kierkegaard, *The Sickness unto Death,* trans. with introductions and notes by Walter Lowrie (Garden City, N.Y.: Doubleday & Company, Inc., 1954), p. 154; Clement quoted in C. G. Jung, *Aion: Researches into the Phenomenology of the Self,* vol. 9, part II, R. F. C. Hull, trans., 2nd ed. (London: Routledge & Kegan Paul, 1968), p. 222.

[2] William Glasser, *The Identity Society* (New York: Harper & Row, Publishers, 1972).

[3] Lewis Carroll, *Alice's Adventure Under Ground* (Univer. Microfilms, Inc., 1964), pp. 49-50. A facsimile of the original Lewis Carroll manuscript.

[4] Robert Coles, *The Middle Americans: Proud and Uncertain.* Photos by Jon Erikson (Boston: Little, Brown and Company, 1971), p. 3.

[5] Peter Schrag, "The Forgotten American," *Harper's Magazine,* vol. 239, no. 1431 (August, 1969), pp. 27-34.

[6] Coles, *op. cit.,* p. v.

[7] Francis Wickes, *The Inner World of Man* (New York: Holt, Rinehart and Winston, 1948), p. 66.

[8] Rasa Gustaitis, *Turning On* (New York: Signet Books, 1969), p. 221.

[9] Wickes, *op. cit.,* p. 59.

[10] Charles A. Reich, *The Greening of America* (New York: Random House, Inc., 1970), p. 156.

[11] Erik H. Erikson, *Insight and Responsibility: Lectures on the Ethical Implications of Psychoanalytic Insight* (New York: W. W. Norton & Company, Inc., 1964), p. 94.

[12] Robert Coles, *Children of Crisis: A Study of Courage and Fear* (Boston: Little, Brown and Company, in association with Atlantic Monthly Press, 1967), pp. 46-52. Copyright © 1964, 1965, 1966, 1967 by Robert Coles.

[13] Coles, *The Middle Americans,* p. 5.

[14] Rollo May, *The Meaning of Anxiety* (New York: The Ronald Press Company, 1950), p. 252.

CHAPTER TWO

[1] Robert Coles, *The Middle Americans: Proud and Uncertain*. Photos by Jon Erikson (Boston: Little, Brown and Company, 1971), p. 95.

[2] Aniela Jaffé, "Symbolism in the Visual Arts," in Carl G. Jung, ed., *Man and His Symbols* (London: Aldus Books, 1964), pp. 247, 248. Photograph of painting by Vasily Kandinsky, SEVERAL CIRCLES, No. 323, 1926, permission of THE SOLOMON R. GUGGENHEIM MUSEUM, New York.

[3] Paul Tillich, *Systematic Theology: Existence and the Christ* (Chicago: University of Chicago Press, 1957), vol 2, pp. 45-61.

[4] Soren Kierkegaard, *The Concept of Dread*, trans. with introduction and notes by Walter Lowrie (Princeton: Princeton University Press, 1957), pp. 30-32, 47.

[5] Albert C. Outler, *Psychotherapy and the Christian Message* (New York: Harper & Row, Publishers, 1954), p. 103.

[6] *Ibid.*, p. 111.

[7] Herman Melville, *Moby-Dick or, The Whale*. Edited with an introduction and annotation by Charles Feidelson, Jr. (New York: The Bobbs-Merrill Company, Inc., 1964), p. 121.

[8] Shirley Jackson, *Life Among the Savages* (New York: Farrar, Straus and Giroux, Inc., 1953), pp. 85-86.

[9] George Jackson, *Soledad Brother: The Prison Letters of George Jackson*, intro. by Jean Genet (New York: Coward-McCann, Inc., 1970), p. 55.

[10] Gerhard Von Rad, *Genesis: A Commentary*, John H. Marks, trans. (Philadelphia: The Westminster Press, 1961), pp. 72-73.

[11] Bernhard W. Anderson, *Creation Versus Chaos: The Reinterpretation of Mythical Symbolism in the Bible* (New York: Association Press, 1967), pp. 30-31, 37.

[12] See James B. Ashbrook, *Humanitas: Human Becoming and Being Human*, chapter 6, "Some Human Tools" (Nashville: Abingdon Press, 1973). Copyright © 1973 by Abingdon Press. Much of the material in the rest of the present chapter comes from *Humanitas*, chapter 8, "What Makes Humans Human?" and chapter 9, "What Are We Up Against?"

[13] Harry M. Orlinsky, ed., *Notes on the New Translation of The Torah* (Philadelphia: The Jewish Publication Society, 5730-1969), pp. 49-52. I am indebted to James Astman for this reference. See also Ernst Cassirer, *The Philosophy of Symbolic Forms*, vol. 2: *Mythical Thought*, Ralph Manheim, trans. (New Haven: Yale University Press, 1966), pp. 94-104; Erich Neumann, *The Origins and History of Consciousness*, vol. 1, R. F. C. Hull, trans., Bollingen Series 42 (New York: Random House, Inc., 1954), p. 104.

[14] Anderson, *op. cit.*, pp. 81-82.

[15] Alan W. Watts, *The Two Hands of God: The Myths of Polarity* (New York: George Braziller, Inc., 1963), p. 49.

[16] Von Rad, *op. cit.*, p. 74.

[17] Soren Kierkegaard, *op. cit.*, pp. 26-27.

[18] "Recent embryological research has demonstrated conclusively that the concept of the initial anatomical bisexuality or equipotentiality of the embryo is erroneous. All mammalian embryos, male and female, are anatomically female during the early stages of fetal life. In humans, the differentiation of the male from the female form by the action of fetal androgen begins about the sixth week of embryonic life and is completed by the end of the third month. Female structures develop autonomously without the necessity of hormonal differentiation." Robin Morgan, ed., *Sisterhood Is Powerful: An Anthology of Writings from the Woman's Liberation Movement* (New York: Random House, 1970), p. 226.

"Along with forty-seven other chromosomes in the male body cell, there is one tiny one, called the Y-chromosome. . . . [It] has a negative function: when a Y-carrying sperm fertilizes an ovum, it simply reduces the amount of femaleness which would result in the formation of a female fetus." Germaine Greer, *The Female Eunuch* (New York: McGraw-Hill Book Company, 1971), p. 16.

[19] Joseph Campbell, *The Masks of God: Occidental Mythology* (New York: The Viking Press, 1964), p. 106.

[20] G. Ernest Wright and Reginald H. Fuller, *The Book of the Acts of God* (Garden City, N.Y.: Anchor Books, Doubleday & Company, Inc., 1960), p. 56.

[21] Von Rad, *op. cit.*, p. 79.

[22] Rollo May, *The Meaning of Anxiety* (New York: The Ronald Press Company, 1950). See chapter 2.

[23] Harvey Cox, *On Not Leaving It to the Snake* (New York: The Macmillan Company, 1967), p. xiii.

[24] *Ibid.*, p. xvii.

[25] John Macquarrie, *An Existential Theology: A Comparison of Heidegger and Bultmann* (New York: Harper & Row, Publishers, Harper Torchbooks, 1965), p. 87.

INTRODUCTION AND CHAPTER THREE

[1] Theodore Roszak, *The Making of a Counter Culture: Reflections on the Technocratic Society and Its Youthful Opposition* (Garden City, N.Y.: Doubleday & Company, Inc., 1968), pp. 233-234.

[2] David Bakan, *The Duality of Human Existence: An Essay on Psychology and Religion* (Chicago: Rand McNally & Co., 1966), pp. 102-153.

[3] Especially today with heightened consciousness, it is presumptuous at least and partial at best for a person in one group to write *of* the experience of people in other groups. I as a white and a male can only write *about* blacks and females. I do so on the assumptions that (1) within our differences lie human commonalities, and (2) my own wholeness requires the inclusion of others' life and light. I am especially indebted to Emma Trout and Maxine Walaskay for their input and insights related to being an i as a woman.

[4] Rollo May, *Love and Will* (New York: W.W. Norton & Company, Inc., 1969).

[5] Robin Morgan, ed., *Sisterhood Is Powerful: An Anthology of Writings from the Women's Liberation Movement* (New York: Random House, 1970), pp. 36, 549-550.

[6] *Ibid.*, p. 377.

[7] U.S. Current Population Reports, Series p.-60, Consumer Income, 1972. Tables 49 and 50.

[8] Morgan, *op. cit.* p. xxvii.

[9] *Ibid.*, p. 360.

[10] *Ibid.*, p. 378

[11] *Ibid.*, p. 381.

[12] *Ibid.*, p. 236.

[13] Calvin S. Hall, *The Meaning of Dreams* (New York: Dell Publishing Co., 1961).

[14] Ira Progoff, "Waking Dream and Living Myth," in Joseph Campbell, ed., *Myths, Dreams, and Religion* (New York: E. P. Dutton & Co., Inc., 1970), pp. 176-195.

[15] Germaine Greer, *The Female Eunuch* (New York: McGraw-Hill Book Company, 1971), p. 11.

[16] Bakan, *op. cit.*, pp. 120-124.

[17] Robert Coles, *The Middle Americans: Proud and Uncertain.* Photos by Jon Erikson (Boston: Little, Brown and Company, 1971), p. 8.

[18] Susan Sutheim, quoted in Morgan, *Sisterhood Is Powerful*, p. 496. Copyright © 1969 by *Women: a journal of liberation*, 3028 Greenmount Avenue, Baltimore, MD 21218.

CHAPTER FOUR

[1] Sidney M. Jourard, *The Transparent Self* (New York: Van Nostrand Reinhold Company, 1964), pp. 46-55.

[2] Charles A. Reich, *The Greening of America* (New York: Random House, Inc., 1970), p. 288.

[3] *Ibid.*, p. 30.

[4] *Ibid.*, pp. 239-240.

[5] Alan W. Watts, *Psychotherapy East and West* (New York: Ballantine Books, 1961), p. 196.

[6] Jourard, *op. cit.*, p. 54.

[7] James Baldwin, *Nobody Knows My Name: More Notes of a Native Son* (New York: The Dial Press, 1961), pp. 9-10.

[8] Graham Greene, *The Potting Shed: A Play in Three Acts* (New York: The Viking Press, 1957), p. 123. Copyright © 1957 by Graham Greene. Reprinted by permission of The Viking Press, Inc.

CHAPTER FIVE

[1] Betty Roszak and Theodore Roszak, eds., *Masculine/Feminine: Readings in Sexual Mythology and the Liberation of Women* (New York: Harper & Row, Publishers, 1969), p. 304.

[2] Howard M. Halpern, *A Parent's Guide to Child Psychotherapy* (New York: A. S. Barnes and Company, Inc., 1963), pp. 15-17.

[3] Irenaeus in *The Early Christian Fathers*, Henry Bettenson, ed. and trans. (London: Oxford University Press, 1958), p. 106 See also Stephen Charles Neill, *A Genuinely Human Existence: Towards a Christian Psychology* (Garden City, N.Y.: Doubleday & Company, Inc., 1959).

CHAPTER SIX

[1] Fritz Perls' famous dictum: losing one's mind and coming to one's senses. See also Bernard Gunther, *Sense Relaxation Below Your Mind: A Book of Experiments in Being Alive* (New York: The Macmillan Company, 1968); Frederick S. Perls, et al., *Gestalt Therapy: Excitement and Growth in the Human Personality* (New York: The Julian Press, 1951); William C. Schutz. *Joy: Expanding Human Awareness* (New York: Grove Press, Inc., 1967), and *Here Comes Everybody: Bodymind and Encounter Culture* (New York: Harper & Row, Publishers, 1971); John O Stevens, *Awareness: Exploring, Experimenting, Experiencing* (Moab, Utah: Real People Press, 1971).

[2] The following exercises were developed by Dr. Larry Kroeker, Dr. Robert Pellegrine, and myself in 1969, drawing upon a variety of sources such as those in note 1.

[3] Joen Fagen and Irma Lee Shepherd, eds., *Gestalt Therapy Now: Theory/Techniques/Applications* (New York: Harper & Row, Publishers, 1971), pp. 140-149. Also see Frederick S. Perls, *Gestalt Therapy Verbatim*, compiled and edited by John O. Stevens (Lafayette, Calif.: Real People's Press, 1969).

[4] Fagen and Shepherd, *op. cit.*, pp. 205-212. Reprinted by permission of the editor and publisher from Frederick S. Perls, "Dream Seminars" in Joen Fagan and Irma Lee Shepherd (ed.), *Gestalt Therapy Now*, Palo Alto, California: Science and Behavior Books, 1970.

[5] Medard Boss, *Psychoanalysis and Daseinanalysis* Ludwig G. Lefebre, trans. (New York: Basic Books, Inc., 1963), pp. 5-27, figures 1-5. Used with permission.

CHAPTER SEVEN

[1] Charles Williams, *The Descent of the Dove: A Short History of the Holy Spirit in the Church* (London: The Fontana Library, 1939), p. 48.

[2] Gerald Sykes, *The Hidden Remnant* (New York: Harper & Row, Publishers, 1962), p. 209.

[3] Joseph Jobé, *Ecce Homo* (New York: Harper & Row, Publishers, 1962), pp. 128-129.

[4] Erich Fromm, *You Shall Be As Gods: A Radical Interpretation of the Old Testament and Its Tradition* (New York: Holt, Rinehart and Winston, Inc., 1966), p. 59.

[5] Paul Tillich, *The Eternal Now* (New York: Charles Scribner's Sons, 1963), pp. 26-35.

[6] Meister Eckhart, *A Modern Translation*. R. B. Blakney trans. (New York: Harper & Row, Publishers, 1941), p. 232.

CHAPTER EIGHT

[1] Figure 3 and adaptation of Figure 5, pp. 24 and 26, *Individual Behavior*, revised edition by Arthur W. Combs and Donald Snygg (Harper & Row. Publishers, 1959). Used by permission.

[2] Frederick S. Perls, et al., *Gestalt Therapy: Excitement and Growth in the Human Personality* (New York: The Julian Press, 1951), pp. 27-28.

[3] Rollo May, *Love and Will* (New York: W. W. Norton & Company, Inc., 1969), pp. 174-175.

[4] See James B. Ashbrook, *be/come Community* (Valley Forge: Judson Press, 1971), pp. 21-34.

[5] H. Westman, *The Springs of Creativity*, with an introduction to Part Three by Sir Herbert Read (New York: Atheneum, 1961), pp. 123-125. I am indebted to Dean R. Wright for bringing this book to my attention.

[6] Everett L. Shostrom, *Man, the Manipulator: The Inner Journey from Manipulation to Actualization* (Nashville: Abingdon Press, 1967), pp. 67-68.

[7] Theodore Roszak, *The Making of a Counter Culture: Reflections on the Technocratic Society and Its Youthful Opposition* (Garden City, N.Y.: Doubleday & Company, Inc., 1968), pp. 143-144.

[8] Milton and Margaret Silverman, "Psychiatry Inside the Family Circle," *The Saturday Evening Post*, vol. 235, no. 28 (July 28-August 4, 1962), p. 46.

[9] Westman, *op. cit.*, pp. 128-130. Used with permission of Niedersächsishes Landesmuseum Hanover.

[10] *Ibid.*, pp. 126-128. Illustration reproduced with permission of British Museum.

[11] May, *op. cit.*, pp. 124, 126.

[12] Kenneth B. Clark, *Dark Ghetto: Dilemmas of Social Power*, Foreword by Gunnar Myrdal (New York: Harper & Row, Publishers, Harper Torchbooks, 1967), p. 78.

[13] Jürgen Moltmann, *Theology of Hope: On the Ground and the Implications of a Christian Eschatology* (New York: Harper & Row, Publishers, 1967), p. 162.

[14] "Perhaps the most important single fact that the human intellect has yet discovered" is that "all ideas are partial." Yet one of the dangers of our age, more damaging than any time previously, is "total obsession with partial ideas." Lancelot Law Whyte, *The Unconscious Before Freud* (New York: Basic Books, Inc., 1960), pp. 7-8.

[15] Hans Selye, *The Stress of Life* (New York: McGraw-Hill, 1956), p. 246.

[16] Soren Kierkegaard, *The Sickness unto Death,* trans. with introduction and notes by Walter Lowrie (Garden City, N.Y.: Doubleday & Company, Inc., 1954), p. 177.

[17] Ernest L. Rossi, *Dreams and the Growth of Personality: Expanding Awareness in Psychotherapy,* Pergamon General Psychology Series (N.Y.: Pergamon Press, Inc., 1972), p. 74.

INDEX

Acedia, 38-39, 65

Adam, 36-37. *See also* Polarities

Antony, St., 97

Anxiety, 25, 38, 68-70, 118

Apathy, 39. *See also* Acedia

Aquinas, St. Thomas, 49

Augustine, St. 30, 31

Awareness: 35, 37, 67-68, 98; of self, 66, 94; sensory, 87

Baldwin, James, 67-68

Becoming, 20, 27, 54, 71, 119

Being, 26, 27

Black experience, 23-24, 32, 48

Body, 52, 87-91

Breathing, 89, 91

Carroll, Lewis, 13

Christ, 75, 81, 86, 91, 98-100, 103

Clement of Alexandria, 11

Coles, Robert, 23-24

Complexity, 35-36, 91-92

Concupiscence, 39

Conflict, 18, 28-30, 91, 94

Consciousness, 35, 37

Courage, 94

Cox, Harvey, 38

Creation, 33, 34-37

Creation Story, the, 32-33

Cross, the, 20, 114-116

Crucifixion, 76, 99-100, 102

Daniel, 112

Darkness, 35, 52

Defense, 17, 38

Denial, 113-114, 117

Depth, 34, 51

Desert, 20. *See also* Wilderness

Desire, 31, 39

Dream, the, 34, 37, 49-50

Dreams, specific: cows and ocean, 92-94; head of 57 committees, 22; Joan's, 50-55; pass self around, 23; potting shed, 70; raft, 69

Eckhart, Meister, 105

Emotions, contact, 112

Eve, 37. *See also* Polarities

Faith, 117, 118, 119

Fear, 114, 117, 119

Felicitas, 97

Feminine principle, 52, 55-56, 93-94

Figure/ground, 109-110. *See also* Gestalt

Freedom, 37

Fromm, Erich, 10, 102

Garden of Eden, the, 36-40, 111

Gestalt, 92, 119. *See also* Figure/ground

God: 33, 34-35, 36, 38, 81, 96, 105; image of, 49; knowledge of, 11; nature of, 62, 75; providence of, 119; revelation of, 49

Greene, Graham, 70

Greer, Germaine, 56

Growth, 17, 18, 19, 20, 21, 26, 38

Guilt, 65-66

Heschel, Abraham, 9-10

Hillel, 83

History, 33

Hubris, 38-39, 65-66
Human, genuinely: 58, 74, 98-99, 103, 119; predicament, 27-32, 37, 60; situation, 13, 32-33, 40
Humanity, 18, 36, 40
i, 10, 34, 37-38, 46, 49, 56, 64-65, 68, 75-81, 86-87, 94, 98, 102, 119-120
Identification, 105
Identity: 13, 17, 21, 43, 64, 85-86, 105; crisis of, 24, 38; disturbed, 23; limited, 19
Irenaeus, 75

Jackson, George, 32
Jackson, Shirley, 31
James, William, 97
Jesus, 25-26, 46, 62, 98, 112, 117, 118. See also Christ
Jonah, 112, 118

Kierkegaard, Soren, 11, 30, 37, 118
Knowledge: 17, 37; of self, 11

Language, 28
Liberation: 43; human, 73-74; men's, 59-60; women's 45-46
Life, 20, 24-25, 32, 33, 34-40, 100, 101
Light, 35, 37
Love, 28, 44, 75, 98, 103
Luther, Martin, 31, 32

Man, a, 59-71
Masculine principle, 52, 55-56, 93-94
May, Rollo, 10, 110
Men, 67
Moses, 111

Narcissus, 39
Nature, 33
Negative, the, 52-53, 119
Neil, Stephen, 10

Old me, the, 25, 27, 28-32, 34, 40, 46, 52-53, 56, 62-64, 67, 68, 69, 86, 88, 97, 102
Order, 34-35, 100-101
Original sin, 28-32
Outburst, 101, 108. See also Polarities
Outler, Albert, 30, 31

Participation, 87. See also Polarities
Paul (apostle), 22, 31, 102, 103, 119
Perception, 108-110
Perls, Frederick S. (Fritz), 92-94
Perspective, 108, 118. See also Gestalt
Polarities: 36, 96, 103, 108, 109-110;

Adam/Eve, 74; elder boy/younger son, 62, 74; Martha/Mary 46-47, 74; outburst/order, 9-10; spontaneity/regularity, 9-10
Prayer, 9-10
Pride. See also Hubris

Racism, 25, 30, 111
Reich, Charles, 23, 64
Relationship, 35, 97
Relaxation, 88-91
Responsibility, 38, 70, 100-101
Risk, 103-105, 117-119
Roszak, Theodore, 41
Ruby, 23-24, 109

Savior, 119
Self, the: 11, 17; birth of, 36; centered, 28, 94-95; full, 10, 67; image of, 24; lost, 20; seeking, 51; split, 13, 26
Self-centered, 28, 40, 100
Self-consciousness, 39
Self-disclosure, 70
Selfhood, 37
Self-transcendence, 97
Serpent, 37, 111-112, 114-117
Sex differences, 43, 93-94
Sexism, 25, 111
Sin, 30. See also Original sin
Son of Man, 114, 117
Spirit, 103, 118
Split, 74. See also Human: predicament; situation
Strange(r), the, 87
Symbol: Egypt, 111; lion, 70, 110, 116; wholeness, 52. See also Serpent; Tree

Tillich, Paul, 10, 30, 104-105
Transformation, 94-96, 110, 119. See also Figure/ground; Gestalt
Tree, 20, 37

Unfaith, 39

Von Rad, Gerhard, 36
Vulnerability, 102

Watts, Alan, 66
We, 98
Wholeness, 38, 81, 100, 107, 117, 119
Wilderness, 111, 117, 118
Will, 44, 56-58, 103-104
Woman, a, 19, 23, 45-58
Womb, 36, 40. See also Garden of Eden
Women, 19, 56

Yes, 119-120

Index of Scriptures

OLD TESTAMENT

Genesis
1   27, 32-35
2-3   27, 28, 32-33,
            35-38, 40
4:1-8   28
4:9   60
6:5-7   28
9:20-21   28
11:1-9   28

Exodus
3:14   33
20:5-6   30

Leviticus
19:33-34   87

Numbers
21:4-9   111-112

Ecclesiastes
7:29   27

Isaiah
11:6-7   85
30:6   111

Jeremiah
1:9-10   118

NEW TESTAMENT

Matthew
5:48   118
7:24-27   25

Mark
2:23—3:6   101
5:1-20   25-26, 91
5:9   13
10:15   101
12:28-34   97

Luke
4:13   117
9:57-62   103
10:38-42   46-47
15:11-32   62
17:33   97

John
3:14-15   114-116
10:10   96
10:18   101
13:3-17   98
15:15-17   98-99

Romans
1:18-23   27
3:9-20   28
6:4   43
6:5-11   102
7:21   118
7:25   110
8:28   119

1 Corinthians
1:27-28   119
3:21-23   91, 97
6:19-20   87
10:12   22
12:7   97
12:14-26   119

2 Corinthians
1:19-20   120
5:17   38, 86

Galatians
2:18-21   103
2:20   83, 98
3:28   75

Ephesians
2:13-18   86
2:15   85
4:13   75
4:18   66

Philippians
2:4-8   102
3:13-14   107

Colossians
1:16-17   91, 107
3:10-11   86

1 Thessalonians
5:23   85

1 Peter
2:7   119

2 Peter
3:10-13   103

1 John
3:2   103

Revelation
20   117